Published in 2018
by

Content Writer
Workshop

ContentWriterWorkshop.com

KINGMAKERS

A CONTENT MARKETING STORY

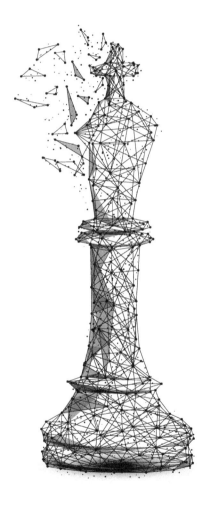

DAVID J EBNER

THANK YOU

Any success I can claim began with these people listening to some far-fetched ideas:

Cathy Strayhorn

Laurel Jean Ebner

Shaun Geary

Connor Holmes

Steve Howell

Cameron Kennerly

Matt Reinstetle

Phoebe Brown

Tony Garcia

Immanuel Jones

Jeremy Daniel

Maves

Karen Flaherty

Gary Corriston

Karen Brown

Jason Ockert

Stefan Kiesbye

Fred Maglione

Introduction

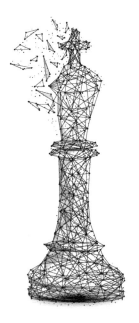

Here we are: two people searching for answers in the same place. The only difference between you and me is where we find ourselves today, at this very moment. For me, it's 2017 and I'm recovering from being lost. I've been traveling down an irregular path secluded from the drum beaters of the marketing world for some time. I haven't fit in with most of my fellow marketing coworkers over the past few years, and this book, along with many other things, is an explanation of why I think that is.

This book is a manifesto—sure. But not in an arrogant, self-inflating way. It's more like shouting self-deprecating truths into a dark abyss. I'm here for a departure from that nonsense and to tell you about my journey for as long as your patience persists.

First, a bit about how I came to this place with you, then we'll chat about your story.

My journey started as a freshman at Kent State University. Not the main campus. I attended the often over-looked (and rightfully so) regional campus in Canton, Ohio. In my first-year English class, we had to read a book of fiction and write an evaluation about some element in the book.

The book: *Slaughterhouse Five* by Kurt Vonnegut, and it made all the difference. Prior to that point, I had written a terrible collection of short stories called The Austin Boys. Don't Google it. You'll find nothing. But my creative writing interests were piqued during high school. However, writing and photography (my other high school passion) were not lucrative career choices. So said my father.

I was studying mass media communications. I was going to be a radio personality… because, you know… radio was assuredly a thing that would stick around in prominence.

A few pages into *Slaughterhouse Five*, a thought seared in my mind. I thought, "What a load of shit." Not Vonnegut, of course, but society, norms and my dad telling me to seek a lucrative career. Here's a guy writing about a time-traveling WWII private, optometrist and alien sex slave. Here he is, and it's magical. Lucrative is shit. Emotion rules! Content is King! Content creators—Vonnegut and the like—are the kingmakers, and I wanted to be among them.

No matter the subject matter of the content, anything that can entice a conjured empathy through words or images—the arts—that's where I wanted to be. That's the magical piece that makes everything of any success level move.

Blue hair, face piercings and aliens, soak up the shine, because the sun is here for you. Just give us some feeling.

I got a "C" in that class, but instantly changed my major to creative writing. I wanted to make people feel. I wanted to lift people off the page with transcending emotion.

By the time I finished my undergraduate studies, I had moved to Tampa to attend the University of South Florida. One more truth found me just after graduation. My father died.

It was a difficult time, and the details are something not pertinent to the conversation, except for the single truth that he was right. Creative writing is not a lucrative pursuit for most.

I sold running shoes for a while, then was lucky enough to land a consulting gig in Atlanta for my Fraternity, but for a huge cut in pay. However, these struggles hardened the thickness of my Neanderthal skill. And, in a move that can only be described as pure vanity, I returned to Tampa to attend the University of Tampa, an overly expensive institution of higher education (as almost all are), and studied… you guessed it, more creative writing.

I was going to be a novelist, or a professor, or something equally as noble and troubled.

My skull started to thin a bit when money became harder and harder to grasp. But a guy whom my wife used to work with mentioned a job opening for a copywriter at a medical marketing firm where he worked.

Both my then-coworker, as well as my wife, soon exited my life in splashes of scandal and ignorance. But I propelled forward. I was a writing fiend, a regular soul-selling fiddler of words and Search Engine Optimization (SEO) and landing pages and collateral.

I finished graduate school and in the nights, as I rested in bed alone and full of the days' carnivorous word salad, I told myself that I may seek a PhD or apply for adjunct professorships. When each new day dawned, however, I was a vicious competitor of words once again.

I wrote more than my coworkers and my content performed. I was fueled by engagement. Every click, every landing page heat map, every lead was a tick in the win column. Before long, the wins started to consume the vacant space reserved for the losses. Move over, blank column— winners are here to devour you.

I rented a small room in my fraternity brother's home and lived a fairly minimalistic lifestyle, but the money was good.

I wrote a script that was selected to become a radio commercial. Then our team was awarded an American Advertising Association Gold Award for collateral. Shortly after, I was promoted to Content Manager and started adding members to my content team. Great writers, the entire lot, but most had little marketing experience. That didn't matter; what did I know about marketing anyway? All I knew was that people enjoyed reading good content. I didn't know it at the time, but this was a novel concept with most in the marketing realm around me.

I was promoted again to Content Strategist, a position I fabricated at my office because I knew how much it would pay if I ever sought to leave the company for an equitable title elsewhere. I kept making more money. Yet, the story was starting to slow. A "road work ahead" sign floated softly in the distance. When a coworker that had previously made comments defining her lack of perceived value for content got promoted to be the Marketing Director, I knew it was time to exit.

For a bump up in pay but a move back down to a Content Manger position, I took on a new gig. How'd I sell myself? I wrote a blog. That's all. It was the first of its type I'd ever written. But a previous supervisor turned me on to the concept of influencer marketing referrals through list-based articles (listicles) and I winged it.

It didn't take long for me to realize that this new gig was just a waypoint on a longer journey. During a 3-month period, we only completed one campaign. An email with 4 blogs linked out. Every piece of content I wrote was edited by people who had less content marketing experience than I did, who insisted on changes based on their personal preference rather than any actual objective reasoning. After a dozen rubber stamps, I was left with terrible content that better resembled the CliffsNotes of War and Peace than anything of value to the reader.

But I had learned of one valuable tool over those three months: marketing automation. I took certifications and educated myself on the ins and outs of value offers, inbound lead generation, buyers' journeys and, most importantly, personas.

Have you ever heard a new idea or philosophy and gave you the feeling that it was something you had always known to be true, yet you were hearing of it for the first time?

It harkens back to foundational truths. When we transpose the essence of a foundational truth—the DNA of the thing—onto some other equation, we have these moments of epiphany and don't really understand why. That's what happened to me.

My foundational truth was that people engaged in stories, not words, and definitely not products. It's what I discovered while reading Vonnegut all those years prior. It's why I became a writer and subconsciously ditched my path to professor-hood for a career in marketing. I wanted to help people, not to get them to buy something or convert necessarily, but to have a shared experience with them. I wanted to write to change thought, action and subsequently the world around me. With fiction and poetry, that shared experience can be pretty isolating, and often years pass before you know how your writing affected others—if you ever know. With marketing, I can write a blog and the moment I hit publish a reciprocal flow of emotion returns to me in the form of clicks, comments, shares and downloads.

When I read about personas vs. demographics, it all came together. Bam! People don't engage based on age, race, gender, location or the mediums through which they see something. They engage because of their motivations. These motivations are often emotional and predicted by their behaviors.

I love the board game Monopoly, but few of my siblings will play with me anymore. I'm a bit too competitive. I see the whole board and strategize 5, 6, 13 moves ahead. I make deals that end in the demise of the other players way down the line. They don't trust me. I'm alone often. However, it always amazes me that, no matter the circumstances, the race car is one of the first tokens to be snatched up. Sometimes, a fight ensues over the piece.

Why? It's flashy, sexy and feels new. Which piece is never divisive? The thimble. It's plain, a known standby and hasn't evolved in centuries.

Many marketers fall into either the race car or thimble camp. They get distracted by the new shiny untested marketing channel or they hold true to the old standby that ultimately starts to wither. Think Snapchat vs. Email in the digital space. I reject both camps. I only follow the behavior, no matter the channel, no matter the unlikeliness of success. You can read the newest articles or dive into PEW research, but the behaviors of your specific persona never lie.

I took my new understanding to an interview with a financial technology company that sold services to fraternities and sororities. I knew the CEO personally. He was looking for someone to lead the marketing department and shift them toward an inbound, analytical approach and away from the historical practice of datamining conducted by sales reps, followed by ice-cold sales calls. Oh, and he wanted the candidate to have a depth of knowledge about greek life on a professional level.

All truths being told here, there may have been 5 people in the entire world that had that specific combination of skills. And even now, I wonder if those were the skills he was looking for or just what I perceived I could offer to him. Nonetheless, after flying to Georgia and presenting to a room of people from varying backgrounds, I got the job.

This is where I find myself today. I left out a few details. Somewhere in there I was hit by a car and my long-standing belief that I am Superman incarnate was reaffirmed. I also fell in love with one of the copywriters I hired. Not that situational type of love where someone you spend a bunch of time with grows on you. No, it was like first-sight-and-I-don't-care-if-it-cost-me-my-career type of love. Pain followed in both instances, but in both, I bounced back.

Here I am, still in the little room at my Fraternity brother's house, making twice as much money as I did when I moved in with nothing enticing on which to spend it.

I'm not bragging. I'm not always happy. I'm driven, though, and these are the things that drive me. That's my story. It's messy, but it's made me agile, and I think it has served me well.

Take a moment here. Think about your story. Go through the steps that have brought you to this place with me.

Here's my idea: Why don't we multiply our efforts by teaming up? Create a pact? We can take a stance that the devil shall not tickle our feet apart, but together as one unit that seeks the light of truth.

Very few of us are competing. And in most channels, you can gain far more by expanding the entire market than carving away at the same slices as your competitors.

I'm going to share more with you in the pages hereafter. I hope it's helpful. I hope you have epiphanies of foundational truth. But mostly, I just hope you don't feel like you're shouting into the abyss anymore. At least not alone.

Where Art
Meets Science

come from an art background. I have a Bachelor's degree in English and a Master's in Fine Arts degree in Creative Writing. I never thought I'd create something that held commercial value. And if you had the opportunity to read my graduate thesis, you may agree with my confidence in this outcome. It was my collegiate dream to piece together an existence upon my intellect as a teacher and the patronage of some wretched souls who found my often-dark writing entertaining.

Six months prior to finishing graduate school, I got my first job in the marketing community as a copywriter. At first, it was just a gig to pay the bills. Then it became a way for me to make money while I wrote. Finally, it became my late-night mistress and my morning coffee.

I'm not the only writer that has had this transformation. Enormous corporations and marketing firms are now targeting creative writers to transition into writing marketing copy. Some companies want creative writers so badly that they're rebuilding their company culture and workplace environment to better attract the artistic personalities of most writers. With the call, "You'll get paid for your writing… finally," writers are moving to join the marketing world.

CREATIVE WRITERS IN A MARKETING WORLD

Content is now king. Truthfully, it always has been. However, content has taken on a new form. Marketing was once heavily laden in terrestrial advertising in the major ad agency days of billboards and newspapers. Now marketing is primarily digital. It's not measured in the macro elements of increased revenue, but instead boiled down to the micro engagements like webpage heat maps, bounce rates and clicks.

The evolution of measurement has also shifted the type of content we deliver to prospective customers. With customizable analytics that can measure a specific user through a journey of website visits, clicks and opens, giant and costly billboards, no matter how grand, seem flat if you're laser focused on conversions.

Let's say you're the Director of Marketing for an omni-channel (single brand) in-house team. It's your explicit directive to provide the company's sales team a certain number of qualified leads over the year, quarter, month, week and even every day. With the pressure that mounts in such an environment, you need to look at multiple pieces of data to decide where to spend your money and how to turn visitors into readers, readers into leads and leads into qualified leads.

In this very common scenario, you start at the goal and work backwards. Let's say you need to supply 4,380 qualified leads a year. That comes out to 365 per month, about 84 a week and 12 every day. Focusing just on the daily goal, you know that every lead you get has a 50% chance of becoming a qualified lead. This means you need 24 leads a day to reach the goal, if 1 out of every 1,000 visitors to your site becomes a lead. Now, you need to attract 24,000 visitors to your site every day. But wait! You notice that if someone subscribes to your newsletter or to receive regular content like a blog from you, they are twice as likely to become a lead! You notice that when someone returns to your site more than 4 times, their likelihood to become a lead is also amplified.

Trends are starting to form, and the crystal ball that is everything but objective says that the more people engage in your site the more they convert. How do people engage in your site? The analytics tell you that they are reading blogs and they are downloading eBooks and using calculators, all of which are helping the reader answer questions important to them. These are things that could make their lives easier or subjectively better.

So what do you do?

Well, if you're like every marketer that has ever been in this position, you start producing more of what works—you double down on what drives conversion.

That's why content is king. In this age, with how conversion is measured, producing more content means getting more leads.

Damnit, How Do Creative Writers Fit into This?!

Ok, if content is king and you know you need more content, the first thing you do is find out what type of content converts the best. It's the content that's not just well written, but composed with the reader in mind, with voice, and feels like a story. It's content that's empathetic to the reader and his or her plight. It's content that provides value to the reader.

All creative writers set out to accomplish a single, very basic, yet very difficult task when they write, and that's to build a shared emotional experience with their readers. They want them to feel something specific. They want empathy.

Creative writers have a box filled with tools that have been honed over years of trial and failure to accomplish the single goal of creating empathy. They build worlds and characters and backstory just to move the reader to an inevitable joint cathartic moment of emotion.

Creative writers have been training to write marketing content ever since they began writing. For most of them, even the recent college graduate, it's a skill set decades in the making.

Where Two Worlds Collide

If applied appropriately, all of those tools, the honed skills, can be used to write marketing content that converts visitors into readers and readers into subscribers and subscribers into leads at a faster and cheaper rate than any other marketing channel.

SKILL VS. EXPERIENCE

This age is further smelted with gold for marketers who've discovered the foundational truth that in any space where skill surpasses experience, profit resides.

Nearly all creative writers struggle to get even their best pieces published or recognized, let alone get paid for their work. They take subscriptions and free copies as payment. In many cases, they pay publishers to read and consider their art for publication.

I'm a perfect example of this conundrum. I've had a few pieces of fiction published over the years, but not many. And I've never received payment for my art. In fact, I've spent thousands of dollars in reading fees and contest submissions just for the pleasure of having others consider my art.

My graduate studies, although immeasurably valuable to me on multiple levels, was a very expensive exercise in paying people to read and respond to my art. So when I received my first paycheck for copywriting, I was ecstatic and this foundational truth became apparent to me.

Since then, I've taken that truth and based my entire career upon it. I grew in the ranks on the back of my ability to write in an empathetic way, and when I was given the chance to build my own content team, I hired creative writers. They were less expensive to employ than people with a marketing background, and they were better at their jobs to boot.

Since then, I've specifically hired people who have a set of skills needed to accomplish my company's needs and have forgone the typical indicator of success through experience.

FARTS

I think it's fair to say that farts are universally hated. Poll your friends and family. Ask your significant other. No one likes farts.

Farts make for bad marketing as well.

As creative writers make the transition into a marketing world there is one giant hurdle to overcome, and that's the concept of art for art's sake.

I have this crude and true idiom that I share with the creative writers on my team that goes something like this:

"A piece of art that doesn't convert gets an 'F' and becomes a Fart. No one likes farts."

I also use this one:

"Art that doesn't convert is like dropping a fresh ice cream cone on the hot pavement. All that excitement and love that could have been; paradise lost."

This was a difficult hurdle for myself as well. When I first started out, I held form and technique too close to my heart and I inevitably wrote some stinkers that I thought were beautiful, but turned out to be very stinky farts.

My past team even wrote fictional stories about our brand around the holidays. We'd use the plight of our readers as horror stories around Halloween and composed carols with interjections of our brand at Christmas. They were terrible. But it was our way to keep the art alive.

It wasn't long before I realized that art and the conversion did not need to be mutually exclusive. They could live together in a single piece. Small elements of art can be used inside of content in ways that actually help drive conversion. It can be done through customer stories or testimonials. Elaborately intertwining story and brand even made for great print advertorials.

In the end, it was the science—the analytical components of marketing—that helped drive content, and it was the art form—the creative word choice and storytelling—that drove conversion.

This collaboration between art and science evolved into something very simple. I call it creativity in a box. We could create whatever art we wanted as long as it fit into this box that was shaped by our end goals. This concept is not much different from the confines that most creative writers face every day. When submitting to periodicals and magazines for publication, there are commonly sharp submission guidelines. Often, these guidelines are things like maximum word count or certain formatting parameters, but more often than not, they contain specific themes that must be present in the piece. Publications like to produce themed content to drive more like-minded readers. Even experiential artists face the confines of physical elements like gravity or the strength of steel to hold up a sculpture or the amount of available space.

In marketing, artists are given the chance to create something that impacts the lives of viewers immediately and deeply. It can drive emotion just as a piece of fiction or a painting can. And all of this can be measured in a microscopic way. All of this emotion can be returned to the artists. They can build the foundation of a career upon it.

Voice vs. Tone

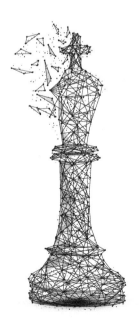

As I pried open my laptop one afternoon to write the words you now read, an old friend of mine sent me recordings from a lifetime ago. In the years just before we became men and knew nothing of the world but the ecstasy of adolescence, we were in a band. It was the most joyous time of my life and I believe the springboard for my aspirations to write fiction and inevitably seek the life of a content marketer.

I played bass, and although I was a novice at best, I was encouraged by my bandmates and I made up a needed piece of the whole. We wrote together, we had creative license to mark the sound with something of our own, and although we quarreled over this note or that lyric, we inevitably reconciled all differences in a call for what was best for the collective whole, the band.

A band, such as the one I was lucky to be a part of, is much like a brand. When you bring a group of artists together, you'll get a cacophony of beautiful sounds, images and words. But the inherent nature of art is that it represents personal emotions and feelings. Every writer, as an artist, has a voice, the small shade of a person that represents their essence personified.

However, every brand has a tone, or what I like to think of as the emotional impression that is left on a person when in the presence of the brand. This can manifest through using the brand's products, talking to others about the brand or engaging with the brand through an intermediary.

So the great content marketing paradox is posed: How can artists maintain their unique voice when applied to the general tone of a given brand?

VOICE OF THE WRITER

Art is an outward representation of the internal struggle of a person's feelings for things that are fundamentally fleeting. This truth extends into the writer's work and helps develop a voice. A writer's voice is a pride-filled characteristic.

Voice can be exposed through many different artistic choices by a writer. Some may believe that it comes down to thematic elements or common motifs in work, but I believe it is far more granular. Genre and theme speak to content, but they don't speak to uniqueness. There are no original thematic elements. Billions upon billions of stories have been written and told in the history of humankind. If you believe that your voice is developed around such elements, then you are simply not unique.

Arrangement and word choice are what create emotion. It's certainly not sexy sounding, but it could be if the right composer holds the baton.

There are more than 1 million words in the English language. That's far and above the most out of all the written and spoken languages in the world. It's the largest tool shed in the universe for any artist. Writers use these tools to display specific shades of emotion throughout a text which, when combined and ordered in a certain way, create a rollercoaster of emotion for the reader. During certain times, the hills and embankments are soft and offer no immediate danger to the reader. In other instances, a writer can use these tools to build great peaks and valleys that take the reader on a treacherous journey of constant peril or love. And of course, a great writer can do all of this with various combinations that showcase the entire spectrum of emotion.

We're not all great writers, but we can all develop a voice, and with 1 million tools at our disposal, we certainly can develop a unique one.

TONE OF THE BRAND

All brands are trying to sell something. That's the goal, even if that thing is a feeling or mission and not a physical product. Many brands are simply trying to trade their valuable content for your attention. This is how media companies make money through advertising. For example, basic television is free to consume as long as you have the means to receive the signal through the airwaves. They make money by garnering your attention through valuable content like T.V. shows and then sell little bits of that attention to advertisers.

Yet even in these cases, success comes down to offering value. To get their foot in the door of your attention and time, they need a brand.

Branding comes down to constancy. This is where a company develops a reputation. That channel is known for more family-oriented programming, and that other one is known for sex-oozing dramas, et cetera.

To build a brand, you must produce products, value and even write content in a consistent manner. This constancy builds the reputation of the brand and creates a comforting feeling for those who consume the brand. When consumers feel comfortable with such consistency, they buy more, they buy more often and they become raving fans of the brand.

After years and even decades of producing content in a consistent manner, a brand develops a tone—an impression upon those who consume it.

Trust is built over time and destroyed in singular moments of inconsistency. It's not surprising that companies hold their brand in high regard and protect it at all costs.

But in a world of developed brand tones, how do artists, those people with the storytelling skills to build shared emotional connections, still create content that doesn't dilute their unique voice?

T-Mobile's Approach to Brand and Voice

If you haven't engaged with the T-Mobile brand in recent years, it has taken an interesting path. In 2013, the company was fresh off a blocked merger with AT&T that would have made it part of the largest telecommunications network in the world. They were falling behind Verizon, Sprint and AT&T in market share.

At this time, T-Mobile decided to become a disruptive brand in their industry. They launched their "Un-carrier" marketing strategy. They no longer were going to handle contracts like the other big brands. Additionally, they started allowing people to pay for phones over two years and they allowed you to use roll-over minutes. Moreover, they started marketing to the rebellious youth of America that didn't want to be tied-down in a traditional cell phone plan.

Today, nearly every carrier offers contract-free plans and unlimited calling. Both of these harken back to T-Mobile's ingenuity. The T-Mobile brand continues to maintain a rebellious tone in their marketing strategy.

T-Mobile Brand Interview

Thought-Horizon is a marketing and social selling agency in Atlanta that works with T-Mobile to help their sales team produce individualized organic content to build their brand.

I had the great fortune of chatting with Matt Apesos, the former Vice-President of Sales and Operations for Thought-Horizon, about the T-Mobile brand and the unique challenges such a brand faces when you need to introduce individual voices.

> **David:**
>
> After working for some time with T-Mobile, how would you define the tone of their brand?
>
> **Matt:**
>
> Over the past few years, T-Mobile has grown into a household brand. A major part of that is because their marketing leadership has focused on defining exactly what the brand stands for. T-Mobile can clearly articulate what their brand is and what their brand isn't.
>
> T-Mobile's brand has historically been consumer focused. This presents a real challenge for their B2B Marketing efforts. Trendy, hip, and slang usage might convince a college student to buy one phone, but the same messaging doesn't appeal to the CTO of a fortune 500 company looking to roll out 50,000 phones to her workforce.
>
> The B2B brand tone at T-Mobile is a more refined version of its consumer brand tone. Flexible, scrappy, and a little bit edgy is the best way to describe it. While Thought-Horizon did not create the tone for the brand, we had to operate within the guidelines.
>
> Developing a voice that matched both the tone of the B2B brand and the tone of the individual sales representatives was tough. Here's how we did it:
>
> Think about a simple 2x2, with one axis ranging from Professional to Casual and the other axis ranging from Serious to Funny. T-Mobile for Business falls squarely in the Casual and Funny quadrant.
>
> **David:**
>
> Does this tone apply better to certain types of content over others?
>
> **Matt:**
>
> Most people would intuit that the answer is yes, but our research at

Thought-Horizon came up with the opposite result.

We ran several experiments where we took content whose voice was at all points from the 2x2 I described above, and we matched it to social posts (tweets) that also had different tones.

Then we asked people to review the posts and the content and tell us what their perception of the overall tone was. We found that the overall perception wasn't influenced by the voice we used; the perception depended on the audience.

Parameters such as age, familiarity with social media, and career level directly influenced how people perceived the voice of a post. The content was wrapped in the context of the persona, not particularly the voice.

For example, non-social natives tended to see everything as casual / funny because they weren't used to seeing professional / serious information in such a format. Those who we classified as executives tended to also classify posts as professional /serious because that's what they wanted to see (confirmation bias). It was the whole, "I'm a hammer, so everything I read looks like a nail to me" thing.

David:

Are there any challenges for writers trying to develop authorial voice under such a strong brand?

Matt:

Yes, the marketing department. Marketing wants to closely control this to keep the brand as consistent as possible. Unfortunately, a major challenge is that even people within the large marketing departments don't always agree if something is "on tone" or not.

Another challenge is that brand leaders don't want the audience to be able to distinguish who the author is of a brand's message. Brands change creative agencies all the time, and leaders are very skilled in making sure there is a seamless transition.

Now, in terms of long-form content, it might be good to have different authors write different pieces. We experienced that content performance generally was biased towards some authors while others didn't do as well. This was true even when all content was marked as authored by the brand. So performance was grounded in good content and not authority.

After an analysis to uncover the reason, we didn't find much difference in the content other than authorial style… i.e. leading with prepositional phrases, some transitions, and the "cute factor." All factors of the writer's individual voice.

David:

Where do the opportunities lie for creative writers in such a space?

Matt:

I look at it as if the creative writers are no different than actors. Can I pull you in, give you a made-up persona through which to write and you do a good job? Can you assume the role given to you and do a convincing job?

Some creative writers can, others can't.

I have found that some creative writers are so stuck in their own style that they can't (or worse, refuse to) change because they believe their way is "better." In the content marketing space, that is a sure way to fail. (I would argue that this mindset is also a sure way for creative writers to fail in their artistic projects as well.)

In my opinion, the best authors are those who can observe all kinds of people and get into their minds and literally "become" those people as they write. William Falkner is probably the best known for this talent. If you can't become the persona behind the brand… if you can't filter each of your clients through their own brand "lens," then how can you convince your own readers that your characters are dynamic?

Writing content for a brand is a great exercise for any writer. The depth of knowledge that a writer can offer is very useful for a marketer who doesn't usually have that knowledge. For the writer, the interaction with the marketer can teach a different way of thinking about how to express an idea or concept. They are two skill sets that complement each other well.

Also, a good writer can add an extra little something (the 'je ne sais quoi') that makes a brand's messaging stand out. In a way, the writer is creating the soul of the brand. Without the soul (without the creative writer), the brand messaging comes across as lifeless and robotic.

Matt's insights are not unique to the T-Mobile brand. A writer's voice can be their saving grace in the content marketing world, but too much rigidity can sink their success. I've worked with dozens of writers and some can make this jump while others can't.

This quagmire is not unique to content marketing either. Even when writing fiction, poetry or nonfiction, a writer who doesn't have agility will produce works that are stagnant and feel formulaic. Imagine characters all having a similar voice through dialogue? After a few pages of character staleness, things start to become robotic, just as Matt mentions concerning brand messaging.

CREATIVITY IN A BOX

As I mentioned, one of the idioms that we commonly used during my time with the medical marketing firm was "Creativity in a Box." The general concept is that we can bring our own flavor of creativity to projects as long as they play by the rules. It's like a writing competition that seeks a specific theme or has a prompt. You could submit the next great American novel, but if you don't play by the rules, you'll be disqualified. Sure, what you created was artful and beautiful, but it can't be used for its intended purpose. Content writing is the same way.

For most brands the box will take on a couple forms. The first form will always be conversion. If you create a stick-figure, fart-joke comic as the next big branding push for your company, you'll likely have a meeting with your respective supervisor. However, if those damn stick figures sing and dance viewers to become customers, it won't likely matter.

I'm aware that this is only half-heartedly true. This is because the second box is brand. If your fart jokes are on brand and the tone lines up, then great. If you venture off brand, even though you're driving revenue, it may not be the manner in which the company wants to make money. Although, if you drive enough revenue, you may want to discuss repositioning your brand as the "fart joke" brand in the marketplace.

Create pieces of art and flex your creative muscles, but do it in the confines of the brand. It's a challenge, and I am of the belief that art isn't great unless it is challenging to create and even a little challenging to comprehend. If there's no work involved, then there is no risk and your context disappears.

Context Is Why Art Has Meaning

As I mentioned previously, art is the outward representation of the internal struggle of a person's feelings for things that are inherently fleeting. This may be pining for a past lover, or fear of losing a particular struggle, or maybe even hate toward a certain situation. All of these things are grounded in a subjective feeling that's projected upon a limited amount of time. The feeling is often love, and the time represented by death, but that apex of human emotion is to be explained in another book by a more-qualified writer.

As a content marketer, you can leverage your voice as the feeling of a piece. Slap your love on your writing. It doesn't matter who your audience is; they'll enjoy beauty when they see it. Give them what makes you unique as an artist and writer. Don't devolve to the average. Instead elevate the reader to be the exception.

Think of the fleeting nature of the content to be that of brand tone. Not in a negative way, but as a challenge. You're challenged to make a piece of art that is contextually relevant through its ability to be simultaneously beautiful and fulfill the tone of your brand. Oh, and if it converts people, that's great, too.

ONE FINAL THOUGHT

Think of it this way: The brand is going to create content, so why not make it beautiful? People are searching for answers, so why not delight them with the response? Someone is going to write the content. Why shouldn't it be you?

There are two acceptable answers to all the above questions: "Damn straight!" Or, "Because I can't."

Three "E"s

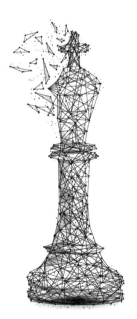

I'm a bit of a movie nerd—not a movie buff so much. I'm lost when it comes to film trivia, but I enjoy watching movies. More than that, I enjoy experiencing movies because I love immersing myself in stories.

It's the same feeling I get when deep into a thrilling book. The thing with books, though, is that real life becomes too much of a distraction to my escapism. If I hear an odd noise or someone walks past me, I'm taken out of the trance and whipped back to reality.

Books are also limiting because they use words to tell a story instead of images and sounds. We attach symbols and emotions to specific images that cause us to feel a story much stronger. A book may take dozens of pages to garner the same effect a movie can in seconds.

Yet, books offer an even deeper escape because of the details. When you read Walt Whitman or Emily Dickenson describe a scene in nature, you're feeling every slight variance. In a movie, there is no possible way to quickly derive those individual characteristics.

It's a conundrum. Which form is superior? Silly question. We are extremely lucky that we don't have to answer that question. We get both, and our imaginations aren't limited by one form.

What about for content marketing?

Video holds the ability to attract us and encapsulate our full attention quickly, while the written word entrances us with precise information.

Luckily, like in the entertainment world, in marketing we don't have to choose. We get the best of both. Words can give us the education we seek and video the entertainment.

But I want both in each form. Because I have one saying that sticks with me and my current team quite readily: Everything, all at once.

I really liked the HBO miniseries Band of Brothers and its companion series, The Pacific. Both shows are based on nonfiction books, memoirs and interviews. And I think that's part of the reason they successfully build a shared emotional experience with their viewers.

Another reason why the shows are so successful is that they hit every point on my "everything, all at once" checklist that all content should aim to accomplish the Three "E"s and be entertaining, educational and engaging.

THEORY OF THE THREE "E"S

During my time with the medical marketing firm I had the pleasure of building an entire content team. I chose to hire five individuals that were all classically trained writers. Four of them had creative writing backgrounds, two had master's degrees in creative writing and the odd person out was a journalist. All were artists.

All five joined the team in a fairly short period of time. This meant hours and hours of training. And who was going to do that? It's not like there was a manual for creative writers to apply their skills in the marketing world.

I had to come up with some quick points that they could fall back on if they got into a pinch with a specific piece they were mulling over. This is where my FART and Ice Cream idioms come from. **Side note:** I'm from the Midwest—we have idioms for everything, and there will be a number still to come in this book. Appease me.

The Three "E"s of content were another quick go-to I shared with my team. All pieces of content need to be entraining, educational and engaging, and in that exact order of importance.

ENTERTAINING

As an artist, I'd like to think that the art that I put out into the world, in whatever shape it takes, is grounded in more than just entertainment. However, the content marketing world does not have such altruistic benchmarks.

When I'm working with graphic artists, I often tell them that when distributing a piece of content on social media, it's the image that pulls in viewers first. People see something beautiful and they want to explore it. By explore it, I mean for about a second. That's when we blast them with some killer short content that entices them to click on the link and read more. But no matter the content, it's that first instinct of attraction that makes them start on the path of engagement.

It's this same intrinsic reaction that makes us engage with content that is entertaining. Our attention span isn't too short. It's just too valuable. Why read something that isn't entertaining? We're not doing research for a thesis. We're engaging with the everyday world looking for snippets of value.

So all pieces of content, no matter the medium or size of perceived value, need to first and foremost entertain their audience.

In Band of Brothers, this isn't a difficult hurdle to overcome. The show is set during WWII on the battlefields of France, Belgium and Germany. Trees are exploding from German artillery, bullets zip across the screen with tracers that make me think of the blasters in Star Wars.

As the series develops there are plenty of entertaining elements. I think, given the setting and subject matter, no one stopped production to ask, "Do you think this is entertaining?"

But as marketers, we need to ask this question. No matter the subject, it's the first of the Three "E"s that we need judge our work against. This isn't to say the piece must be fun or exciting, but it needs to have an element of escapism that all good art does.

EDUCATIONAL

Most of the value gained from content is through the retention of some new knowledge.

We often happen upon a piece of content because we have a question we seek to answer. Maybe we search for it online and look something up in a book (let's be honest, we don't do this anymore). We are constantly seeking knowledge in all its forms.

This is where all the value is contained in content marketing. If a piece doesn't have hearty value for the consumer, then we've not just lost a visitor, we've degraded our brand.

We want people to see our logo in all the places we sling it, whether that's our website or on a Frisbee, and we want them to think, "I trust that Frisbee because I trust that brand. I trust that brand because every time I'm looking for an answer and happen upon their site, I find what I'm looking for."

Think for a moment about how valuable information is.

During graduate school, I was lucky enough to score an interview for a copywriting position. I dabbled by writing some freelance pieces here and there, but I really had little knowledge about what I was doing. I was selling a bill of goods that didn't exist in many ways. I was a year away from graduating and working at a golf course for $9 an hour.

The job posting noted a required skill "knowledge of SEO best practices."

I had heard the term extensively, but I didn't have a good grasp of what the concept meant. A day before the interview, I did a quick search for SEO on Google. Kind of ironic to search what SEO means, but nonetheless, I dove in.

I found a website called Moz. They had a comprehensive beginners guide to SEO, and it was free to download! I was in heaven. I printed out the PDF and went mad with a highlighter. After 12 hours and multiple consumed pages, I was utterly lost. I read dozens of novels as part of my graduate studies. Most of them I annotated and whipped up pages of notes to submit to my professors, but I had an extremely difficult time comprehending this simple SEO guide from Moz. The terminology was foreign and the foundational concepts were beyond me.

I memorized a few points and identified some buzz words that would be easy to recall when prompted. I decided to just keep things short in the interview and act confident, but not seem like I'm not willing to ask questions when I don't know something.

I don't remember much from the interview, but they hired me so I must have said something right. The one thing I'll never forget is how valuable I considered the knowledge I needed about SEO in that moment. It most definitely played a major role in the outcome of that interview, and if it wasn't for that job, I'm not sure I would've ever gotten the chance to learn everything I have about content marketing. I most certainly would not be where I am today without that piece of educational content being available to me.

Now, little did I know it at the time, but when I downloaded that content, Moz put me into their marketing funnel, and although it took years to capitalize on me, I eventually bought a subscription to their services. That entire journey started with me seeking answers and finding Moz as a reliable source. When it came time to consider solutions for my SEO needs, I sought them out and bought their product.

This was also a point in time that I became familiar with Rand Fishkin, the founder of Moz. I owe that man and his vision my entire career, or least that's a feeling I often have, so what's the difference?

Back to our Band of Brothers analogy. The series is designed to be an accurate depiction of the experiences of Easy Company of the 101 Airborne during WWII as told by the men who were there.

The story isn't designed to be educational in the sense of relaying facts of history. It seeks to provide emotional knowledge of those events and the experiences of those men. We watch and keep watching because that emotional knowledge connects us with the characters. When a character makes that final full act of devotion and gives his life, we feel it.

We leave the experience of watching the series with a better understanding of war itself and the toll it takes on the very bravest of our brothers and sisters. In the end, we feel that we're indebted, not just to the men that fought, but the makers of the series and the brand it represents. Because of them, we've gained a level of knowledge that may have otherwise been lost.

ENGAGING

Our content is entertaining with humanizing elements that build a repartee between our brand and the reader's thoughts. We've used all the tools in our artistic shed to give our reader an escape from distractions. Additionally, we've packed the content with educational pieces that add value to our audience's life. After reading our piece they will have leveled up in this specific area of interest.

What more could we ask of this content? It's just words and images.

This is the part that differentiates traditional art from marketing. This is where the science part of marketing kicks in. As previously discussed, all art for marketing's sake needs to fit in the box of conversion. Remember the ice cream on the pavement. This is it.

All content must be engaging. That's not to say it needs to pull in the reader—we've established that with the element of escapism felt through entertainment. We need content to engage a reader to the point that they interact with the content.

This can take a lot of different forms. The most heightened level of engagement would be a form fill of some sort on the website where the viewer saw the content. However, there are a many levels of engagements.

In order of lightest touch to heaviest, here are a few points of engagement:

- **Click through:** This literally just means they clicked on something within your content that is a link to something else your brand produced. It may be an internal link in your navigation or maybe it's a link to an external site you plugged into your copy.

- **Comment:** An individual that adds a comment on a blog is a visitor who likely read the complete article and now seeks to engage the author or other readers. This shows someone seeking to share their emotional experience with the content.

- **Share:** All well-formatted content will have social share buttons along with an email share button to entice those who wish to push the content to people publicly or privately. This is the reader giving the content their stamp of trustworthiness. They are hanging their credibility on the content and saying that it is valuable. Now, it's possible but very unlikely that someone shares a piece of content to show people how bad it is, like in a mocking fashion. Why? Because there simply isn't much social clout to gain by dissing on things. Unless you're in middle school and picking on a smaller, much more nervous David.

- **CTA click:** We'll talk more about CTAs and long-form, downloadable content later, but essentially, it's a way to drive people from content with a lower barrier of entry to ones with a much more heightened level. It's what moves visitors to leads.

- **Form Fill:** As mentioned above, this is a pretty intensive engagement. People may be subscribing to get your content sent to them regularly or asking to get more information about your company or the solutions you offer. All are fantastic! The content you produce that causes people to want to subscribe is content worth trying to emulate.

Phone Call/Direct Message: With the proper tracking mechanisms in place, you can measure people calling or messaging your company directly from a specific piece of content. This could be a print article like an advertorial or a piece of collateral like a brochure or flyer. It can even be a piece of digital content. Next to someone driving to your office with a sack of cash to buy your products, this is the most direct and highest form of engagement. Anytime your content helps trigger an immediate connection between your persona and the sales team, it's a big win. If this happens, you're done. Grab a bottle of champagne and take the rest of the week off. Go ahead, tell your boss I said it was okay.

The three "E"s are not designed to make you twist your voice to accomplish company goals. It's a way for you to use your art to drive value for your readers and your company simultaneously. Your company pays you because your content causes people to buy your products. As long as you create your art for the end user and do your best to fit the art into the box that is engagement, you'll be steps ahead and in the right direction, no less.

Keep creating art and keep creating value.

Personas

In the time between composing the second and third chapter of this book, I made my monthly pilgrimage to my company's headquarters in Columbus, Georgia. A meeting was planned to take place during this trip with the caveat that we'd be discussing the future of marketing for our company. The CEO of our company went as far as setting an agenda that included discussing what we "dream" for the future. We'll chat more later about the attributes that make good leaders for marketers, but someone who plans meetings with dream agendas is rare and should be coveted.

I have a dream problem. I do it deeply, and often while awake. Furthermore, I have the problem of sharing my dreams before fully developed. I restrained myself even to my own surprise. However, that didn't limit the discussion that followed at the meeting, which ended with me being promoted to the Vice-president of Marketing, looking to oversee marketing efforts for multiple brands and talks about expanding the future budget to include more staff and more assets.

I'm sharing this to show that the world is shifting for us content marketers. Where once we were shouting in a vacant, dark abyss, there are now a few brave individuals willing to listen and act. There's a home out there, on some distant shore, where the value we offer is accepted, amplified and appreciated.

SHIFTING FROM ADVERTISING TO MARKETING

As the community shifts further away from terrestrial advertising and toward a more digital emphasis that can be measured on a micro level, we're seeing a new relationship between marketing and advertising develop. Before, marketing was used mostly through the scientific endeavor of market research that supported advertising efforts. Marketing was helpful, but seen as more of a thorn in the side of the subjective ad man. It was phycology and sociology—soft science vs. creativity. Now, marketing drives all advertising. Furthermore, advertising has become just a vehicle to achieve the needs of marketing. Traditional advertising is now just one facet of many lead-generating and brand-building channels, and more focus and energy is being placed on new components of marketing like content.

Why?

It more efficiently captures the end goal of building, not just immediate revenue, but long-term company value. Content does this through building a network of followers that are subscribed to the value you regularly distribute on web-based assets like your website, social channels and the like.

DEMOGRAPHICS VS. PERSONAS

This evolution has been heralded primarily by the digital age and the internet, but still echoes back to the soft-science origins of marketing. Today, every marketer should and must be a social scientist and apply those skills to better understand their customers' motivation to buy.

My cousins formed a company many years ago that focused on (in the simplest of terms) design. They didn't only focus on the fundamental aspects of design, but the human elements. They reverse engineered the experience people would have with a product or an environment and designed from the end-user's standpoint. Their results were products like the first computer mouse for Apple's Lisa, the first notebook style computer, a new Pringle potato chip for Procter & Gamble and many more innovative concepts.

My cousins are David Kelley and Tom Kelley, and their company is IDEO.

In one of the many books written by Tom, he describes the Ten Faces of Innovation. Tom's book could have easily been titled: The Ten Faces of Marketing, or better yet, Walden for Marketers. The tagline would be, "Head into the woods, read this book and emerge a marketer."

One of the ten faces in Tom's book is the Anthropologist, and he describes this individual as such:

"The Anthropologist is rarely stationary. Rather, this is the person who ventures into the field to observe how people interact with products, services, and experiences in order to come up with new innovations. The Anthropologist is extremely good at reframing a problem in a new way, humanizing the scientific method to apply it to daily life. Anthropologists share such distinguishing characteristics as the wisdom to observe with a truly open mind; empathy; intuition; the ability to 'see' things that have gone unnoticed; a tendency to keep running lists of innovative concepts worth emulating and problems that need solving; and a way of seeking

inspiration in unusual places."

This passage serves as the apex introduction to the concept of personas.

We all know demographics as the categories of information designed to depict a section of the population. They look something like: 75% of all Americans between 18-25 check Facebook on average 11 times a day.

Have you heard of Personas? Personas are a collection of specific pieces of information which describe a single individual who represents the common or ideal user of your product. Personas include the intricacies of personalities. They look something like: socially driven, urban dweller, goes to Bonnaroo every year.

Where demographics are clouds of information that help us group and quarantine those who usually buy our products, personas allow us to study the personalities of the ideal customer in an effort to map their motivations.

Personas are a further drilldown of people in a demographic. If the demographic is a cloud, then personas are the snowflakes. They are unique yet derive from a common place.

Persona workshopping is one of the best places to start when strategizing for content marketing. Knowing who your audience is can help you better target the emotional connection you want to make. Empathy is as subjective a feeling one can have. The mere definition demands attention to the characteristics that make people unique.

I use demographics to help determine which content distribution platforms may be beneficial to garner the attention of my potential customers. However, personas help determine what content is likely to trigger engagement. This concept will be outlined in more depth in a later chapter where we'll discuss passengers, drivers and vehicles.

CASE STUDY: SUPER-SECRET MEDICAL MARKETING FIRM

Three years ago to the day, the first piece of content I had ever written as a full-time copywriter hit the internet. I was proud, of course, so I shared it on social media and some friends rewarded me with likes and comments. That rush of an emotional connection immediately filled me with excitement to the depths of my toes. But it was a complete FART.

Firstly, the content wasn't written for my friends, it was written for people that suffered from a chronic and terminal lung disease. No matter how beautiful the prose or pleasing the graphics, it needed to garner engagement, and it didn't. That was a good lesson.

It seemed almost idiotic of me to even have shared the blog on social media. Our demographic was 70 years old and essentially dying. Tons of market data showed that our potential customers didn't have social media accounts. In 2014, we were still heavily producing print ads and even some billboards because that's where the data sent us, and it was right. Although expensive leads, print advertisements were the most reliable and highest converting lead channel.

In early 2015, our content team consisted of 3 copywriters. One also took on our press relations and one took on social media posting. The idea of needing dedicated attention to social media was such a ridiculous thought that it was relegated to the more junior member of the smallest team in the marketing department.

By March, new leadership presented the opportunity to pitch the need of a content manager to lead the team. There just so happened to be one of those great marketing leaders across the table, and she said yes.

Once in a role of direction (a very small one at that), I started to cross reference the data available about the common social media user as it correlates to our demographic. Nowhere could I find any information about 70-year-old social media users. Why would there be? The sample pool would be so small it wouldn't be statistically significant to the big market research firms.

During this point in time, a massive influx of advertising dollars was being spent on Facebook for the first time. Result data was pouring in, and everyone claimed to be an expert. Subjective and definitive statements were spreading.

I read about "phantom followers." This was the argument that paying for followers on social media was a worthless endeavor. That if you look deeply into the percentage of followers that engage in content, there was a point of diminishing returns. Through Facebook's algorithm of curated content, people liked so many pages and engaged with so few that your content would likely never make their feed, let alone garner engagement.

Facebook was moving more and more to a "pay to play" platform where you had to boost every post if you wanted to ensure an impression with your followers. As an aside, they still operate heavily in this space today. Many companies spend obscene amounts of money just to garner visibility on social media.

It didn't make sense to me, though. We may have had a couple thousand followers on Facebook at the time, and we were posting about a blog a day. But our organic social reach was a good percentage of our followers, and furthermore, we were getting great click through rates on linked content. But given the size of our followership, the numbers didn't seem significant enough to make a definite determination.

We argued for a measly $300 budget to be used for a followership campaign, and we once again were lucky enough to get a yes.

Our actions progressed from there. We had monthly themed campaigns and were getting followers for $0.5, then it dropped all the way down to $0.25. Compared to the data coming from the experts, we were scoring followers at half the cost of just about everyone else on average.

Fast-forward 2 years and we were pacing for 50,000 Facebook followers. More important were the click through rates. When we posted blogs, we were getting an organic reach in the thousands, and we closely monitored click though. Anything above 5% and we considered boosting.

It came to be that we were boosting multiple posts a week and sometimes a dozen a month. But the secret to all that success had everything to do with 2 major factors.

The first factor was how our Facebook followers were unique. These individuals suffered from a chronic disease for which there was no known cure. They felt alone in the world. Their doctors told them there was little that could be done for them, and they were further ostracized from society due to the physical restraints their disease afflicted upon them. Walking up the stairs or down the driveway could seem like an impossible feat for many of them. The idea of a social life was a doomed dream for most. So these individuals sought to engage with society digitally. Even though they were well into the demographic of people that doesn't use social media, they were extremely active regular users.

Furthermore, they were researchers. They were constantly looking for content that would help them better understand their condition and what, if anything, they could do to improve their health. Also, they didn't quite follow the same social media etiquette rules most of us wouldn't dare compromise. They shared content like crazy. They shared ads even! We'd see them posting tons of their friends' names right into the comments on the post, which drove up relevancy. They liked and loved content daily. They'd take links to our content and share them on their loved one's Facebook walls.

It was like when you accidentally click reply all on an email, but with every email you've ever received, and you've forwarded said email to every person in your digital rolodex.

Secondly, and most importantly, the content we were posting was resonating with our audience. We'd get comments on social media and on our site that inspired tears in our eyes when we saw how much people appreciated our articles. People even called our office referencing the content when they spoke to a sales rep.

There was something special happening with our content—something that the general marketplace filled with its experts and theories would scream to the heavens as impossible. We were garnering qualified leads from a demographic thought to be absent on social media directly on Facebook.

WHAT THIS MEANS

That was a moment that a foundational truth crept into my life. Behaviors, and the motivations that drive them, will always trump what demographic data predicts. The essence of the persona concept is that you should never discount the raw power of content that is written directly to a unique individual with an intentional emotional experience in mind.

I had never heard the term "persona" up to that point, and it would be another year before I had for the first time. To this day, when I'm alone in that abyss and I'm worried about where to go next, I'm often drawn to the memory of those heart-felt comments and the mutual emotions I shared with the comment's composers.

Advocate Marketing

The company I work for was acquired a couple years ago. Since then, we've been acquiring and merging other brands in our space in an effort to offer more solutions to our customers. These customers have priorities set out in their respective missions and are seeking solutions to help accomplish said missions. As good stewards and advocates for them, we're constantly seeking ways to help. Sometimes that just means advice, and in others, bringing the solutions they need into our suite of products can offer even more benefit to our customers.

This reality presents some unique opportunities. Our marketing team is now going to provide services to multiple brands. We're moving more and a more toward an agency methodology. But, all of the brands we service are part of our owned family.

The expansion will also provide us more resources, as well as new marketing venues, personas and opportunities to delight people and foster raving fans. These new brands, however, are established and need to be protected as well as maintained. So where do you even start in a scenario like this?

Content marketing.

THE SPOTLIGHT IS OFTEN WARM, BUT SOMETIMES SWELTERING

Over the past few months, I've been called on to facilitate a presentation about the marketing practices of our brand to both the parent company and the new companies that are now a part of our broader family. It didn't take long for me to realize that I was being asked to provide proof of concept for our marketing team and, though a steep dramatization, my very existence.

As I presented to a handful of company presidents and to the entire executive team for our parent company—something that felt less like a presentation and more like a job interview as the minutes ticked past— there was one section of the presentation during which I felt an air of empathy with the group. It was the section on content marketing.

I had covered analytics, promotions and inbound marketing methodology, but when I got to the blog, the social media and the long-form value content, people perked-up. I like to think that many in the room felt the very same thing I feel when I think of content marketing—the foundational truth that providing value and solutions was exactly why people bought our products in the first place. Doesn't it make sense to amplify that concept more widely?

Most of the brands in the room had not focused intensively on digital marketing or a strategy to propel their brand into the arenas where their potential customers spend their attention—at least not on a mass scale. They've all created a hugely successful business and products based around the value they offer their customers. In turn, those customers gabbed about their experience and referred people to the company. The entire business development model is stoked by the embers of their customers. When they wow more customers, they get more customers. It's a fantastic cycle of delighting people.

When I spoke about doing just that—by adding value for more people through content—they saw it as a direct reflection of how they've built their companies.

Aha!

WORD OF MOUTH (WOM)

What do you call someone who calls your company looking to buy your products because, "So and so at the office/down the street/at a convention told me about what you did for them?"

You call this customer service done right, but you also call it a word-of-mouth lead.

There is no debate on this point, WOM leads are the best type of leads. They are very often bottom of the funnel (BOFU) leads, meaning they are far along in the buying journey. Mostly, this is caused by some angel advocate—the one that told them all about their awesome experience with your brand. No need to nurture these leads from the bare bones of interest all the way along the marketing funnel. No need to then pass that lead over to sales for a needs assessments and value proposition. That's not to say any steps change for your sales team, but some sort of value must be apparent for them to have reached out to you.

WOM is the way most businesses get their first big break in the business development department.

Have you ever asked yourself why companies spend so much time and resources on customer satisfaction? I'm a hopeless romantic-type so I'd like to think it's out of the goodness of their hearts. You know, spread the cheer and warmth of humanity… Nah. Great service has a huge upside for new revenue and helps maintain reoccurring revenue from long-term customers.

This entire mantra has been triggered by those sales early on in the life of the company. Those people called because an advocate was out there preaching the good word about the company.

It works.

WOM Conversion

On top of the relative low cost of getting WOM leads in the door (you can assume all company costs associated with servicing a customer add up to the cost of an eventual brand advocate, but it's hard to attribute those direct costs to specific leads), they close at a much higher rate as well.

That makes a ton of sense, right? If someone comes to your company because of all the awesome things they've heard, they are more than likely going to say yes when you ask them to buy.

A great sales team even leans on the customer that referred the WOM lead. By constantly mentioning that customer and sharing specifics about their experience and how the company helped them, you can continually use the good will you've developed with a happy customer to make your current lead feel at ease. If you're dealing with a raving fan, you may even be able to get them to jump on a call with your sales team and a WOM lead to help push efforts further.

How do you get more WOM leads? Furthermore, as a content marketer, what role can you play in the process?

Digitize WOM

It's pretty easy to hide behind the apparent ownership of WOM leads on customer support, but that's a poor marketing practice. All leads, no matter the manner or path they take to get to your brand, are your responsibility as a marketer.

Hell, if you're going to abdicate any responsibility over leads, certainly don't do it for the leads that have the best conversion rates! Instead, look at WOM leads as an opportunity to gain even more revenue for your company. And you can look to your awesome skills as a content marketer to multiply those efforts.

Through content marketing, you have the ability to digitize WOM. You can now take those watercooler conversations—those beautiful instances when someone that is thrilled with your brand raves about it to their friends—and amplify them with a bullhorn.

Reviews and Testimonials

The most common and easiest way to digitize WOM is through testimonials and reviews. Very often opportunities for testimonials will come directly to you in the form of a phone call or a regular check-in with a customer. Sometimes people will write an email to your company to tell you how your products have improved their lives, and other times that may be a natural conversation during a regular call between your customers and your customer success team. This also may come in the form of social postings and messages or even though a chat application on your site.

You may be asking yourself what all of that has to do with content marketing? Although there will be many modes of communication that touch multiple departments, it's the marketing team's task to use this content to drive leads. And it is, of course, content. Just like a blog or any webpage, these small snippets need to be curated and checked for grammar, garner approval from the customer on the final rendition and be distributed to the masses.

♛ BEST PRACTICES:

- Have a system in place for staff members to submit testimonial comments directly to the marketing team. Maybe a landing page with a form.

- Make sure to collect the commenter's contact info for follow up.

- Collect a picture of the commenter. This is crucial in lending credibility to the testimonial.

- Create a distribution network and, if possible, run ads on the keyword "(your brand name) reviews."

- Lastly, make sure your staff is trained to recognize opportunities to collect the comments and how to facilitate those conversations.

Reviews are a bit of a different beast, yet still play a very important role. These will commonly live on external sites like social media and industry-specific websites. Also, general business review sites like the BBB. This is all content that drives real business development results.

Although the content cannot and should not be curated by you, it's important to still target building a good number of reviews.

♛ BEST PRACTICES:

- Drip email campaigns. Try to hit the inbox of users at a predetermined time just after they should be fully integrated in using the product, but before any perceived honeymoon period has worn off.

- Target people who gave a testimonial. After you've vetted the vast number of people who have said great things about your company, segment them into groups that best match the site where you'd like them to go leave a review. Pick the site where that individual will have the most influence. A CEO may be directed to the BBB while a college student may be directed to social media.

- Pick the one place you think they will make the biggest impact and make a direct appeal. Don't send a message asking them to pick from 5 different sites on which to leave a review. It's much better to be specific with your direction.

- Tools like USER IQ and other net promotor score (NPS) software can automate this on your site directly.

Side note: It's not good ethical practice to incentivize reviews because this can sometimes unintentionally create a subservient relationship between the reviewer and the company. People tend to give you only glowing reviews if they think they may get a reward, even when the opposite is explicitly stated. Likewise, don't ask anyone who is not a customer to leave a review, or anyone with a conflict of interest like an employee. That's just lying, and it's bullshit marketing.

♛

Referrals

Referral leads typically come to you through a hyperlink to your site from another entity's website that is not specifically from an advertisement, social media or a search engine. While WOM leads will commonly initiate through a phone call or direct communication to your sales team, referral leads often springboard from similar efforts but manifest digitally.

In the section on search engine optimization (SEO), we'll chat more specifically about backlinks and their ability to build credibility for your brand and domain strength for your website.

Instead of just using your site as a reference point, some backlinks can be used when directly reviewing your company, your service and your products, which collectively make up your brand.

Keep an eye on sites that review products in your industry. Build a relationship with these sites by writing content about their site and work in a few hyperlinks to their site. Or, contact the site and ask if they are interested in some guest content. Write them a blog that speaks to their broader audience. Usually, it's considered bad form to link directly to your site in guest content; however, linking to your site in the bio section of the guest writer (you) helps.

Most brands, mine included, welcome and greatly appreciate guest content.

Push the Voice of Others

A large component of a successful content marketing strategy is content distribution through brand advocates. This can take a lot of various shapes. The best way to advance your WOM and referral traffic is to build a brand advocate community.

Such a community can manifest in a number of different forms. It could include location-based advocacy teams helping spread the word of your brand and the benefit you can provide people in that specific location. Not unlike street teams, these groups usually have some vested interest in the success of the brand, whether monetary or otherwise.

Another approach is to develop an online community through a forum or social media sites. These communities can act like support groups where people can ask questions about your product, share stories and give you both insight into your brand authority and offer you an opportunity to delight customers.

You could even build an advocacy reward program. Your customers can apply for an "ambassadorship" and as they promote your brand they can be rewarded. As I mentioned before, make sure this doesn't devolve into payment for false testimony.

You'll need to develop terms and conditions for an ambassadorship. Make sure to thoroughly vet applicants and have them agree to not speaking in false terms about your brand or their experience.

There are several solutions available to help you organize and manage a program like this. These solutions include applicant tracking, measuring the effectiveness of your ambassadors and accumulating points that can be cashed in for rewards, raffle entries or discounts on your products.

What do you get in return? Attention. The best way to leverage your ambassadors is through sharing your content. You can prompt them to share posts on social media, participate in online forums and even be a referral for a potential new customer wishing to chat with a current customer.

Sponsored Content

One approach that our team has used is what we call "Adshare." It's not a new concept. We simply ask our corporate customers to allow us to sponsor social media advertisements to their followers.

Sponsored content has been used in content marketing for years. It's extremely effective because the "advertisement" is usually native content that contextually makes sense to appear within your partner's environment.

The more native the content feels the more successful it usually is in attracting referrals to your site. To achieve this, it's best to work closely with your sponsor partner and cultivate the content together. Give them options to help shape the content so it is on-brand for them.

Our social Adshare partners see the added benefit of extended brand exposure through our relationship as well. We build the advertisements, and once they approve, we pay to push the message. The advertisements come from our partner, but it has our content on the page so it's their brand getting exposure. Our benefit is that we have a partner that is sharing content about our solutions to people under their influence.

It's exposure that we would unlikely be able to obtain otherwise, or at least at much greater expense.

INFLUENCER MARKETING

A new and growing field in content marketing, and more specifically content distribution, is influencer marketing.

This has come a long way from the days of brands seeking out people with large social followership and asking them to post an image of them using their products. Of course, there's still a lot of that. Now, there are influencer marketing platforms that are used to manage and cultivate influencers for your brand—much like ambassador programs. The largest difference between ambassadors and influencer marketing is the relationship the advocate has with your company. Typically, an ambassador has an incentive for sharing your content that is not only motivated by money. They use your product, love your product and want to see you succeed. Influencers typically are just in it for money.

You can set a lot of tight parameters around who you accept as an influencer, what they post and how your brand is represented, but it's not a perfect system. There needs to be a level of trust and professionalism involved if you want to make sure your brand is not misrepresented. You can even set tight controls around how influencers get paid. You can pay them only for sales they bring in, or you can incentivize website visits and clicks.

FINAL THOUGHT

No executive will shy away from someone who says, "I'm going to take all the reasons why people buy your products today and multiply those efforts." That's exactly what advocate marketing does.

Curating those WOM experiences and digitizing referrals so that more people can learn about the great things your brand is doing is a winning formula for any content marketer.

"SEO It"

My family owns a small artisan coffee roasting company in Tampa, Florida. It's a passion project that grew and grew and now consumes most of my free time in the best possible way.

However, I'm a mad man. I cannot deny this fact, but it would likely help me greatly if I were to come to terms with it. I run from one thing to the next. I believe that time is valuable, and no one wastes my time more than I do. So I hustle.

In a fit of hustle, I made the poor decision of trying to move a ninety-pound coffee roaster by deadlifting it. I work out regularly and feel confident in my strength, masculinity and prowess, but there was a small yet very consequential factor I ignored, which was awkwardness. That defining characteristic of my youth had returned to wreck me once again.

This roaster is oddly shaped, making it difficult to get a grip grounded for lifting. I came at it all wrong and I paid with a pinch in my lower back. I moved away and stretched a bit. I thought, "That was odd," and like the mad man I am, tried to lift it again. Pain shot through my spine and down my left leg. I felt it all the way down in the tiniest toe on my left foot. I couldn't believe how much it hurt and likewise, how idiotic it was for me to make that second attempt.

So the last three days I've been fairly immobile, in constant pain and dependent on muscle relaxers and pain killers to just function. I've lost hours of productivity. My 8-hour work days have turned into 12-hour days because I'm spending large chunks of time thinking about pain or not thinking at all because of the pain killers. I actually fell asleep during a teleconference with Salesforce!

Additionally, I've not gone to the gym in three days and I'm sleeping 2 extra hours a day due to drowsiness from the muscle relaxers. In three days, this mad man that values time above all else lost 18 hours that can never be regained. Why? Because I didn't think things through? Because I wanted a shortcut that I thought could save time in the end?

This ordeal has put me in a horrid mood, so naturally I thought it was a good time to write about Search Engine Optimization.

FUNDAMENTALS OF SEO

This section of the book will be filled with rants and complaints because

I can't stand how often people get ripped off by marketers that say the 5 erroneous words, "I can SEO your website." They promise traffic and high rankings and all the glory that comes with a business owner seeing their website at the top of a search engine results page (SERP).

SEO isn't a button that's hidden in the depths of your website. There isn't a magic line of code that you can plug in just the right place to kiss your page by the Google Gods.

Think about this for a moment with me. If it were that easy, if there were a way to "SEO" your website and some gorilla marketer knew the recipe for the secret sauce, do you think they would be the only one? That this is the one and only person that stumbled upon this method? Of course not. And if there were a way to do just that, wouldn't everybody be doing it? And if everybody were doing it, would it work anymore? In this crazy scenario, SERPs would be swapping pages at the top every few moments. The top rankings would be a revolving door of websites that have been "SEO"ed by the secret sauce chefs.

If it worked, it'd inherently be its own doom.

Here is a foundational truth for you:

Love is a verb and so is SEO.

Optimizing a site for organic search is a behavior, not a gimmick.

Just like love, it takes time to perfect and it needs to be maintained, reinvented and invigorated on a regular basis. You need to keep at it and never be fully satisfied or complacent.

This wasn't always the approach. Back in the day, people would cram links in carless places and stuff keywords in the footer of their site just to gain ranking, but it didn't take long for Google to fix those glitches. It's been a painful process for some. For those that have been in this game for more than a decade, the way pages are ranked has changed aggressively. And all those tricks will get you nowhere now.

No, to truly SEO a website is to be committed to form, technique and due diligence. It means checking every box on the SEO checklist every time you produce a new piece of content. It means distributing that content out to the world. It means maintaining that content long term instead of hitting publish and walking away. It also means writing a piece of art that fits snuggly into the emotionally empathetic box we call engagement.

SEO means thinking of the viewer's experience first and reverse engineering your content around that point of view. It means all of these things because that's how Google's algorithm works. It's an advocate for your visitor, not your revenue. Google isn't in the business of making more money. If you don't believe this, just take a look at the number of paid search ads on a page today compared to 5 years ago… There are half as many. No, they bank on serving the right content to the right user at the right time. And they know if they continue to do this, they will continue their dominant market share, which in turn will drive the business outcomes they seek.

It's a brave position—to deny guaranteed revenue in hopes to create an even better user experience. But thank the lord Google took this stance. If not, the internet would be the wild west of advertising. Pop ups and paid links everywhere! Articles that have been written by robots to cram in keywords as much as possible. Companies switching out every noun on their website with the name of their latest product!

The Starbucks Cold Brew walked down the Starbucks Cold Brew and met up with Starbucks Cold Brew to execute their Starbucks Cold Brew.

Panic and Pandemonium! Or something like that.

508 Compliance and SEO

Can you imagine surfing the web and not having the ability to see with your eyes? Think about how difficult it would be to find something. How fast would you give up? According to the World Health Organization, there are approximately 285,000,000 visually impaired people in the world.

Section 508 of the Rehabilitation Act of 1978, further strengthened by the Rehabilitation Acts Amendments of 1998, is quoted as follows:

"Technology must be accessible to employees and members of the public with disabilities to the extent it does not pose an 'undue burden.' Section 508 speaks to various means for disseminating information, including computers, software, and electronic office equipment. It applies to, but is not solely focused on, Federal pages on the Internet or the World Wide Web." (www.access-board.gov)

508 compliance speaks to the ability of your site to be accessible to the visually impaired, among others. To accomplish this feat, every nuance of a web page would need to have some sort of tag or que that supplied a visually impaired person with a verbal explanation of whatever is being represented on the page.

A picture would have to have a written descriptor that could be verbally pronounced, and a link would have to have a URL descriptor as well. Meta description now becomes a summary and page titles have way more meaning, as they help define what cannot be readily seen.

If tags and keywords could help a visually impaired person better understand what comes next or what they are experiencing, why couldn't it help a search engine find what you are looking for? Just like a page reader could scan written content and verbally relay the contents of a page, couldn't similar technology scan through content and look at some of those very same tags and match those tags to words you type into Google and then match your search to a page?

Of course it can, and a small portion of most search engines do just that.

My first copywriting job came with a Digital Manager named Gary. He would give us SEO tips on a whim, as if they were afterthoughts of a New Jersey drunkard you passed on the sidewalk. One of those tidbits of wisdom was to write content for blind people. He loved being purposefully crass, but he wasn't wrong.

Side note: Gary would have these SEO review meetings with our content team and he'd go through this long list of things to do to make sure we're hitting all the SEO marks, but at the end of the talk, he'd always say something like, "Just write good shit and it'll preform." He was right about that, too.

KEYWORDS

Keywords are one of the three pillars of SEO. (More to come later. See how I'm leading you on…)

As we know, the best content is reverse engineered with the reader in mind. A good place to start is to know what your personas are searching. More specifically, what are they typing into that search bar in hopes of finding an answer?

It's interesting to note that what they are searching for and what they type can often be two different things, and that's important to know.

Cruises are a great example of this. Let's say you're a fictitious marketer named Karen and you want to go on a vacation. You might search "best cruises." That's kind of a lazy search and Google knows it, Karen. They also know that you've searched "Caribbean cruises" in the past. Actually, you've searched it a lot because you're a workaholic and you get excited about the mere idea of vacation, so now you're a vacation voyeur from your desktop. Google also knows that you live in Tampa based off other searches and, of course, your IP address. So Google serves up content that's for Caribbean cruises that depart from the Port of Tampa.

We're certainly getting better at this. Most people search in what is called long tail keywords. I define this as three or more consecutive keywords that further define your search. So something like "Tampa Caribbean Cruises."

Have you ever looked at the actual URL after you search a long tail keyword? Take a look next time. Somewhere in that crazy chain will be words you typed with a "+" symbol in between the words you actually searched. It becomes a mathematical equation. The keyword "Tampa" equals one thing, but the words "Tampa+Caribbean" equals something totally different. It's not the search results for both keywords, but for the two words combined. You've now taken two things that mean something separately and combined them to mean a third completely different thing.

What would the search result be for "Tampa Caribbean?" Maybe information about the distance between Tampa and the Florida Keys? Or possibly a Wikipedia page about ships departing Tampa bound for Cuba during the Spanish-American War?

However, the search term "Tampa Caribbean Cruises" will likely serve up exactly what you intended: the calm break from the office that you deserve, Karen. Yeah, Karen, I'm singling you out! Go on a damn vacation already!

Why is this important? Karen probably wants to know, because Karen isn't listening to me about the vacation…

It's important to know how your readers search for solutions and how the search engines interpret what they write. No, this is not a promotion for the exercise of flooding the internet with content targeting small variations of long tail keywords.

Understanding what may be served up to people when they search a certain combination of keywords will help you better refine your keyword targets and your content. If your company sells cruises from Tampa to ports throughout the Caribbean, then you don't want to be served up for the words Tampa or Tampa+Caribbean because those people aren't looking for what you're offering. You want the people that are looking for you or your services.

Just like Google doesn't just serve up what people search, they serve up what they think the person is actually searching for, you need to not seek just traffic. You need to seek the traffic for those people looking to find the specific answers displayed in your content. And keyword targeting is a very important component in that endeavor.

Keyword Density

Remember my keyword stuffing example with Starbucks Cold Brew? Don't be that person. Don't cram your content with haphazard words that don't contextually fit. You're a word artist and you have that amazing tool belt at your disposal. Paint a complex landscape using happy little birds as your keywords.

Be the Bob Ross of content marketing.

Where it works in your content, use your keywords. Heck, they are driving the topic you're writing about, so use them! They'll fit in just fine if you're on topic.

A good rule of thumb is to shoot for 1% keyword phase density. For a 1,000 word article, that means using that phrase 10 times.

👑 *PRO TIP:*

If possible, use your keyword phase in these ways:

- Obviously, 1% throughout your article total
- In a header
- In the first paragraph
- It helps to bold it the first time
- As a link in the article
- In your meta description (more to come)
- In alt text (more to come)

DOMAIN STRENGTH

The second pillar of SEO is domain strength.

Think of your content like a jockey. A well-trained athlete will have a higher probability of providing you the performance you seek. The more experience and the more skill, the better the performance.

Now think of domain strength like a race horse. A well-established horse with a track record of good results won't likely give you erratic behavior. It's predictable. The better the past performance, the better the odds become that the horse will win in the future.

When you top a great performing horse with a skilled and experience jockey, it makes for a high probability of success overall.

It's the same with content and domain strength.

You can have the best jockey in the world, but if you place them atop a donkey, it's not going to place in the Kentucky Derby. You can have amazing, artful content that's empathetic and creates a shared emotional experience, but if you post it on a junk website, it won't get ranked.

Building Domain Strength

The strength of your domain, much like the muscles in your body, is developed over time through constant use and peaked performance. To build up your domain strength, you need to produce great content and link to other great and contextual content.

Both inbound and outbound links are a major factor in the strength of a domain. A site with a larger number of inbound links will have better domain strength and Google will give it some props by boosting it in results. The Google algorithm sees websites with a developed domain strength as having more credibility and thus more trustworthy.

Remember, Google's goal is to serve up what it thinks people are looking for. Inherently, if they send someone to a junky site, it's assumed they will have a bad user experience and bounce or click away from the site. That doesn't help Google at all.

How often would you use a search engine that sent you to bad sites?

If you have a lot of inbound links, it looks as though many people see your content as a trusted source. Because that's all a link is, a source to better define an idea or term. A reference.

Outbound links help you build inbound links. Although it should not be approached in quite this manner, it's kind of an "I'll scratch your back if you scratch mine" system.

Websites get notified of link backs. When you see someone linking to your content and their site seems reputable, it makes you want to link to them. It's an exchange of trustworthiness.

So sites with good domain strength that link to your site build your domain strength. If you link to sites with a good domain strength, and produce high quality content, they will likely link back.

Now, don't assume a site like the Washington Post is just going to link to your rinky-dink site because you linked to one of their news articles. It's best to approach sites on your level or just above. It's kind of like the old adage that people want to date or marry someone that they perceive as just a bit more attractive than they are. After you've dated that person, you kind of feel like you've jumped a rung and you're now ready for the next. Adages can be quite superficial.

Link to sites in your league, and then try some just out of your league. Then repeat. It's a slow going process, but just remember what my buddy Gary said, "Just write good shit and it'll perform."

♛ *PRO TIP:*

These types of domains are inherently stronger:

- Government sites .gov

- Nonprofits .org

- Institutes of higher education .edu

- And of course, news entities.

- Secure sites. https://

Typically, sites with user-generated content don't rank as high unless there are a lot of links from them. So sites like:

- Social media (Facebook)

- Forums (reddit)

- Free Sites (davidebneriscool.wordpress.com)

- Sites perceived as not secure

METADATA

The third pillar of SEO is metadata.

Alright Karen, you still with us? Of course you are, you monster, you.

If your amazing content and your beefy domain are your jockey and racehorse, then your metadata is actually showing up to the damn race!

Have you ever seen a horse win a race that it didn't race in?

Meta Title

Metadata describes the small blurb that shows up on the SERP with the URL to your website. It contains two parts: a title and a description.

The title is, well, the title to the content. There are a few different ways to approach meta titles. My good friend whom I've never met and would love to, Rand Fishkin, is the creator of MOZ, an SEO powerhouse. He says you should think of your meta description as a funnel of sorts.

The first thing you should write is the category. So if you we're writing for a blog called "Best of Baseball" and your blog post is about the coolest Cleveland Indians socks on the planet, your title would start out with this:

Socks

Then you would further refine that with a descriptor like this:

Socks-Cleveland Indians

Then furthermore, with your brand:

Socks-Cleveland Indians-Best of Baseball

This model lets you go from what is most important to the reader to why you would trust the writer.

I've worked with companies that prefer their brand come first and then start the description funnel like this:

Best of Baseball | Socks: Cleveland Indians

You may choose this model if you believe it's more important that your brand is seen fist due to the brand identity you've built. Also, meta titles are only so long. They often get cut off so a lot of brands don't like the idea of their name getting axed off the title. Rand would probably say that it's more important that the reader find what they are searching for than know who it comes from. But I don't know, like I've said, never met him… Sad face.

I don't believe that enough of the search engine algorithm veil has been drawn back for anyone to know definitively, but I think both of these options are good practice.

Meta Description

Meta description is pretty straightforward, but seems to get screwed up a whole lot. It's simply the small blurb that describes the page to which the link is referring.

There are only a few rules with meta description: Include the damn keyword, KAREN! And make sure the description accurately describes the article.

You only get about 300 characters, so you can't be too verbose. Be direct.

Some brands like to the end the meta description with the words: "Read More." The whole section of metadata is an actionable link, so with this theory, you'd assume someone might think there is a longer description that may unfold when they click the words "Read More." Instead they'll be taken to the full page on your site. This may lead to unwarranted visits and a high bounce rate, however, so writer beware.

Let's assume the target keyword phrase for our Best of Baseball articles is "Cleveland Indians socks." This is what the meta description might look like:

The Cleveland Indians haven't won a World Series since 1945, but thank goodness the coolest Cleveland Indians socks are now here and, guess what, the socks are actual winners.

If you put it all together, here is your complete metadata in Rand Fishkin's preferred method (in hopes he sees it and calls me):

Socks-Cleveland Indians-Best of Baseball

https://www.bestofbaseball.com/blog/coolest-cleveland-indians-socks

The Cleveland Indians haven't won a World Series since 1945, but thank goodness the coolest Cleveland Indians socks are now here and, guess what, they are actually winners.

LINKS AND ALT TEXT

Back to links for a moment. You already know how important links are, but now let's chat about the best practices for linking.

First, as mentioned, always make your target keyword phrase a link somewhere in your content. It's best to make this an internal link to a page that best describes that term. Maybe it's a glossary type article that is used as a baseline that offers a holistic uncovering of the topic.

👑 PRO TIP:

Make your internal links open in the same window and your external links (those to other websites) open in a new tab or window. This helps boost your average session time for visits and your time on page. Both affect SEO ranking.

Also, remember the term "triangle of awesome links." I have that trademarked but you can use it. Just reference my name right after saying it.

A triangle has three sides, and each side is an element of an awesome link.

The first is the words you actually use as the hyperlink. In the example of the coolest Cleveland Indian socks, assume that it is the target phase "Cleveland Indian Socks." In this case, we'll actually make the target phase, "Cleveland Indians Socks," the hyperlink. That makes up the first side of the triangle.

The second side is the URL that you're linking to. Again, in this case, we'll make it an internal link (opening in the same window) to our catalogue page about all types of Cleveland Indians socks available. The URL for that page is: https://www.bestofbaseball.com/cleveland-indians-socks.

The importance of the second side is that the URL also contains the target keyword phrase, and it will aptly define the term we used as the actual hyperlink in the content, which is also the target phrase.

The last side is the meta link. Remember how 508 compliance relies on tags and cues for a screen reader to audibly relay what items represent? The meta link is just that. It's a descriptor of what the link is. Instead of reading out the URL, it reads the meta link, which is just a simple title for the link. It's also what shows if you hover over a link on a web page.

You sometimes can set the meta link when you build any hyperlink. It's typically in the same screen that allows you to select if a link should open in the same window or a new window.

Best practice in this case would be to use the target keyword phase as the meta link because it describes accurately both the content you are linking to and the URL itself.

Note: Some sites have removed the option to create a meta link. In these instances, the site will usually use the words that make up the hyperlink as the meta link.

So now we have a triangle of awesomeness around this particular link. What makes them awesome is that all three are accurate and connected using our keyword phrase.

All links won't work out perfectly this way, especially if the link is external. You don't have control over the URL structure of another brand's site, but if they are good at what they do—and you wouldn't link to them otherwise—then it'll likely be close.

Alt Text

Alt text is really simple, too. It's just the tag you place on an image.

Anytime you place an image in your content, whether it's a featured image or an image in the body of your content, you have the option of providing a description of the image.

All you have to do is make the description accurate, short and get at least one image to match your target keyword phrase.

You can bet that my coolest Cleveland Indians socks blog has a killer featured image that shows some bomb socks. With this image, I would use "Cleveland Indians Socks" as my alt text.

Alt text, like a meta link, provides a descriptor for a screen reader and also for search results. Have you ever seen an image slider appear in your Google search near the top of your SERP? Google doesn't know what those actual images are, but just like the pages below them, Google ranks them based on a bunch of parameters, one of which is the alt text.

Of course, people also preform searches solely for images.

Alt text is a great way to pull in some extra traffic. It's also a fantastic way to round out your quest to rank profusely on your target keyword phrase.

Do you see a theme here?

Everything tracks back to that phrase being prominent, yet contextual. It needs to make sense. And, to harken back to my old friend Gary, then shit needs to be good.

All right, Karen. Time for your cruise, the rest of the story will be here when you return. I promise.

All Shapes
and Sizes

Art has a subjective audience. It's actually a huge conundrum. If art is subjective, how do we know in the midst of creating something if it will be well received? We may toil through hours of agony and self-deprecating doubt only to create something we believe to be beautiful and others perceive as junk. And speaking from extensive experience in this realm, many artists do.

This leads to a graveyard of art that never sees public life. Many pieces never even get the chance to be judged. Pieces like my graduate thesis. And some pieces, like my graduate thesis, shouldn't really get that chance, because they are objectively not great.

However, when a piece does make it through all of those personal and professional barriers and sees daylight, we need to judge it.

The proverb "let he who is without sin cast the first stone" does not apply to art, nor through intrinsic properties, content marketing.

You need to look at industry content, your competitors' content and even your own content through an objective lens. Don't make excuses. Take emotion completely out of the equation. Easy, right?

This is how you learn and potentially innovate new styles to boost your own skills.

But, the one thing you shouldn't do is criticizes others' content publicly over beers with your friends. Which is what I was doing last night.

I've been known to preach about a huge misstep in the fraternity and sorority industry. No specific organization, or even the trade groups that are positioned to protect and advocate for the community, digitally own the terms "fraternity" or "sorority." There's not even evidence that they are fighting for the terms.

Now, I'll admit that these terms get a ton of news traffic and likely are very difficult to rank on. This is no excuse, however. And now Total Frat Move, the antithesis of a valuable fraternity experience, owns the terms. Don't even get me started on the paid search results.

During this discussion last night, emotions were running high, and a coworker mentioned that there was a company creating content to target those looking to join a fraternity or sorority.

I let it rip! I lambasted the measure as a failed attempt to use content marketing to that end. The only content I saw from this group was bottom of the funnel conversion talk. No real value for the viewer. They weren't even seeking to answer the integral question. Unless their question was, "Should I give you my contact info to sell to other people?" Now, I'm not sure that's what they are doing, but it feels that way.

In my opinion, it looked like they were simply trying to collect leads. I understand this is everyone's end goal, but they're not likely to be successful given their chosen route.

Why?

If every page is a pushy approach to collect contact information and not offer broader value, you will scare off the new visitors to your site, which will never get you returning visitors and the leads you get won't be primed for further conversion. You'll have a bunch of lost puppies.

To own these terms, you need to be seen as the solution provider to the broader question. You need to provide top of funnel content on a regular basis that provides value and answers questions. Think of your audience as coming to you at varying places in the buyer's journey. Many of them are just poking around so give them more than anyone else. And, yes, provide bottom of the funnel content, but it still needs to have value. Don't just ask for a conversion without offering something in return.

This rant enveloped me, and 30 minutes later I stopped myself and backtracked my tirade. The group in question is a well-known and respected partner in the industry and personally I believe they are some the best examples of proper fraternity gentleman and sorority ladies. They just aren't good content marketers.

So, this section is my homage to them and you about the varying types of content you can create, as well as where they fit in the buyer's journey and marketing funnel.

THE MARKETING FUNNEL

Think of the marketing funnel as a tornado. When you start to gain momentum with your content, you'll suck more and more people into the funnel. Once someone enters the funnel, they cannot escape, not because they can't will their way out, but because there is just a very low barrier of entry into the top of the funnel. The mere act of clicking on a link to your site enters them into the funnel.

There are three basic levels in the funnel. Top of the Funnel, or Tofu, is the entrance point. Middle of the Funnel, or Mofu, is the level just below the top and is represented through some heightened level of engagement by the potential buyer. Lastly, the Bottom of Funnel, or Bofu, is the level just before being passed to the sales team as a warmed lead. Again, another level of engagement is enacted to leave the funnel and be passed to sales. This last action represents the highest barrier for marketing materials.

The content marketing funnel is not designed to be categorized by the marketer's level of effort. No, it's categorized by level of engagement needed on behalf of the visitor to consume the pieces of content. This is dictated by a social agreement you make with your audience. You need to match the value of the content you're offering with the value of the ask you make of the viewer. If you ask for a name and email, then they should get your content sent to their inbox regularly. If you're asking for a phone number and to learn more about them, you better offer them something that is worth the assumed time they will spend when someone inevitably calls them. That's the assumption all people make when forfeiting their phone number.

It's a balancing act, but you'll need to test and find a sweet spot where the value of what you ask from them in the form of contact information matches the value they perceive in the content you are giving them offers.

Top of Funnel: Tofu

Your Tofu content is designed to be consumed easily by the reader. No need to dive deep into industry jargon or sell a product here.

This is where most of the mass content on the internet calls home. We're talking content that people can stumble into.

Your goal in this level is to capture website traffic to attach a cookie to your visitor's browser so you can keep a record of their complete engagement with your site. And, if you're lucky, you'll gain a subscriber to your content.

Blogs

Most of your existence as a content marketer will be creating blogs. Why? It's the easiest way to engage a reader and build that shared emotional experience. There is no level of commitment on the part of the reader to view the content. It's also the place where you get to shine. The content can be short and pointed or long and filled with all the skills inside your writer's tool kit.

This is where you'll enact you SEO skills the most as well. Much of the content that will follow in this section will likewise have SEO components, but given that this will make up the majority of content on your website, blogs are your best chance to influence you organic ranking.

Press Releases

News about your company serves a lot of functions. It helps establish company wins. It lets potential and current investors feel more confident in their decisions. Also, it's your chance to brag on your company and your staff. People want to do business with brands they like and make them feel comfortable.

Make sure your press releases are actually news, of course. There is no need to use a press release to announce a promotion unless it is C-level. Don't plan to produce a press release on a regular schedule. You'll end up forcing content into a press mode where it doesn't belong, or you'll fail to meet your editorial deadlines.

It is important, however, to have a mechanism in place to recognize press potential and a regular process to produce press releases quickly. News gets old fast.

Social Media

Social Media serves two very important roles in content marketing. First, it comprises some of the best content distribution channels you have. Secondly, native content on social media is driving up your ability to build a loyal audience.

General copy posts, info graphics and even native videos can all preform on your social media channels well.

There is no lower barrier of entry for engaging with your brand than on your social media pages. They don't even need to come to your site to engage. This makes social media the very top of the marketing funnel.

Nail down a good balance of native posts and those that link back to your site. The worst sin of content marketers on social media is only posting content to drive website traffic, or even worse, talking about your products, too often.

Gary Vaynerchuck has a saying for this, "Jab, jab, jab, right hook." Essentially, he's saying you should give value three times as often as you ask for something from your social media audience. And that ask should be along the lines of visit our website to read this link, not buy our product.

Forums

Reddit is a great example of how a forum can be used for content marketing. Again, very low barrier of entry into the funnel.

As a strategy, you can monitor and interject your brand into conversations about your industry.

Don't monopolize the conversation on a forum! People will get turned off to your brand if they think you're driving the entire conversation back to a rainbows and butterflies vision of your brand.

Be honest and post helpful content. Also, answer questions if it makes sense for the tone of the brand. Think of a forum like a giant search engine where people can ask questions and everyday people answer them. In this scope, you need to consider yourself a regular user and not your company directly.

Don't go crazy with sharing links to your site, but if the content matches the question, have at it.

Testimonials

The stories from your raving fans are the best type of content you can create.

Although you may spend a lot more time and treasure hunting down and developing video testimonials, they still fit in the top of the funnel. As mentioned previously, it's not about work, it's about value.

Since these pieces offer people a direct answer to their questions about what a relationship with your brand may look like, you'll want them to be available for people at any stage in their decision making process. Never put the stories of your customers behind a gateway.

Middle of Funnel

In our tornado analogy, something of good magnetism would need to pull a visitor into the middle of the funnel. You need to get a heightened level of engagement with your content and they need to make some sort of commitment to your brand.

Typically, this happens through a form fill on a gateway landing page. The visitor fills out the form and they get access to the valuable content.

If you write good content, you'll gain subscribers to your blog, but this isn't quite enough to drop the potential buyer down to this level. However, you will get numerous chances to do just that as you push out more and more Tofu content to them.

EBooks

EBooks, when effectively executed, can be some of the most beautiful pieces of art in a content marketer's tool kit.

These long-form pieces of content can cover some in-depth concepts that are important to your personas. Pick topics that are driven by the most searched keywords in your ethos and then further define the content by something to educate your persona.

For example, my persona is a fraternity treasurer that is 21 years old and a junior in college. He is searching a lot about how to engage his alumni in a thoughtful manner to help fund a scholarship for his members. Let's say he searches, "Fraternity Alumni Donations." An eBook idea may be something like, "A Treasurer's Guide to Fraternity Alumni Donations." In this eBook, we'd offer a strategy and a step-by-step process to drive alumni donations.

This level of content is so needed and wanted by our persona that he will likely offer us some detailed data about himself and his business in exchange for a free download.

Templates

Give your personas tools to better execute their jobs and goals. Templates are simple documents that can save your potential buyers time compared to building these items themselves.

This gives you a great space to place you branding, too. Although you may not be able to ask for a phone number in exchange for content this simple, you can likely gain a lot of other data about their business or themselves, which can help you further segment them.

Calculators

Calculators are just plain old fun. People love to play around with theoretical numbers. They are easy to make, too. All you need is a little bit of excel formula knowledge and you're off.

Think about the metrics that your persona would use to measure scalability and success.

For example, my fraternity treasurer is likely constantly thinking of ways to raise more and more funds. He probably has to chase down brothers to pay their dues, which more than likely is just enough to break even. So he may be interested in a fundraiser calculator designed to show how much each individual member of his organization needs to raise to reach a certain goal. You can take it even further and throw some conversion formulas in there. Let's say you expect 80% of your members to attend a fundraising event at a local fare. They are paying you $9/hr for each member who shows up and works a concession stand. And the event is 6 hours. How much money will you have at the end of this scenario fundraiser? Furthermore, if your goal is $$$ for the year, how many events like this would you need to meet that goal?

I'm geeking out a bit because I love calculators. I'm a nerd and if you're reading this, so are you.

Videos

We're not talking about your run-of-the-mill YouTube videos here. Certainly, not testimonials, nor brand promotional videos.

Videos of recorded webinars that cover some sort of educational topic can serve as great Mofu content. This can be a flip through of a presentation about a well-searched topic. The recording doesn't even need to be of a live event with attendees. I've developed dozens of recording of webinars that had no attendees.

♛ PRO TIP:

You can also stage some great educational videos with full studio production value. People appreciate something that's well put together. It needs to feel genuine, so scale back on the formalities and keep the script to how people talk on a day-to-day basis.

I like to write a complete script and give it to a performer and tell them to just say it in their own words. They target specific bullet points and find their own way from one to the next.

Distributing Mofu Content

Place links to your Mofu content using calls to action (CTA) throughout your Tofu content that best matches.

If you write a blog about the top 5 fundraisers for fraternities, it may be a great piece of Tofu content to place a CTA button for our "Treasure's Guide to Fraternity Alumni Donations" EBook, or even our fundraiser calculator tool.

You won't need nearly as much Mofu content as Tofu content. So you can place the same CTA for a certain piece in multiple places on your site.

♛ PRO TIP:

If you use a marketing automation tool like HubSpot, you can even use smart CTAs. This would give you the option to automatically change the CTA to a different version if the reader has already seen and not engaged with another. This is heightened contextual marketing. Being able to personalize content based on the individual person visiting your site can increase conversion in Mofu content greatly.

Bottom of Funnel: Bofu

Here we are, the illustrious Bofu. The power of the winds at the bottom of the tornado are intense. Our goal here is to set a barrier for entrance into the sales funnel which comes next.

After entering the Mofu, we likely have some in-depth knowledge about our visitors. Now we can directly market content offers that meet the visitors where they are in the problem-solving process.

They may be actively comparing your brand's solutions to competitors or just calculating the cost versus value of any type of solution.

Once in the Mofu, the trigger to enter the Bofu is often some level of engagement that proves the lead is looking for a solution. This could be a specific piece of information collected in a form or just engaging in Bofu content.

If they happen upon Bofu content on your site, then great, they just dropped down to that level of the funnel. Outside of this, you may have a nurturing email campaign designed to push Bofu content to Mofu individuals that have consumed some like content or multiple Mofu pieces. Once they engage in the Bofu, they are in.

Solutions Landing Pages

On your site, you should have pages outlining the various solutions or products you offer. Viewing these pages doesn't necessarily enter people into the Bofu. There's really no barrier of entry to this content. However, on a solutions page, you can place a CTA that could trigger a very high level of engagement.

You should also create solutions landing pages. These pages are often a synopsis of the solutions and maybe a video explaining how the solution will provide value to the viewer. These pages will have a form on them to engage even further.

These pages may live in easily accessible points throughout your site or as advertisement landing pages. Therefore, it is very possible that someone who has never visited your site might jump from outside the marketing funnel down to the Bofu and then directly to sales.

♕ PRO TIP:

More than not, leads that skip the entire marketing funnel will close at a lower rate for your sales team and the sales cycle will be much longer. These leads have not developed the same relationship with your brand as those who go through the entire funnel. They didn't have the warming-up period with your content that would establish value in your brand as a solutions provider. So this value building then falls on the sales representative. That's not an effective use of their time. Unless they are a WOM lead, then forget the funnel.

Product Demos

Every brand approaches product demos differently. There is no one best way to engage people with this Bofu content. However, if you sell some sort of software as a subscription (SAAS) then you likely have a lot of leads to cultivate. Or, if your product is designed as an everyday-use type of solution, you may also fit this bill.

You can pre-record product demos that can be viewed by leads on their own and not guided. If you represent a brand that doesn't have an influx of leads to cultivate or your product has varying use cases, you'll likely want these to be guided by a sales rep.

Some brands have gone as far as having ongoing product demos that are very simple and top level, not explaining a specific use case, but just showing some features. You register for a time, but essentially these ongoing demo recordings played on a loop and anyone can dive in when they are free.

These ongoing demos can lead to people registering for a one-on-one demo with a sales rep so they can better answer the question, "How should I specifically use this product to solve my problems?"

Case Studies

If you have a raving fan that has experienced success through using your product, you can develop a case study based off their story.

The formula for a good case study typically starts with building an empathetic connection between the customer and the reader. Try to emotionally relay the negative situation the customer was in when struggling with a specific problem.

Then show the customer searching for solutions. Tell the story of that search and how they inevitably landed on your brand. Maybe they were hesitant to try your brand as a solution and they sought past customers for reference. That's a great story to tell.

Finally, show proof of concept with your solution. Show the customer happy and thriving. Show your customer's reservations about your brand disproven. Show a solution to the problems you presented at the beginning of the case study.

Placing your case studies as a CTA on your solutions pages usually serves very well. Typically, you wouldn't want to place a gateway to this content. You want it to be easily accessible.

So why is it in the Bofu? Because engaging in this content shows a high probability of being a very warm lead for sales. So here's how you move them to solid Bofu ground. Place another CTA in the Case Study content for a product demo. Answer the "how will this solve my problem?" question right after they read about how it solves someone else's problem.

White Papers

White papers are industry-related pieces of content that are bound in research and science. White papers should outline research founded in proven fact. So, even though the topic may be something near and dear to your brand, or even proving the concept of your solutions, it still needs to be approached objectively.

Think about writing those arguments and research papers in college. You chose a side to an argument and you proved it. Even though there are many sides, it's not your job to prove the validity of any argument but your own. Don't negate facts, but don't go down the "two sides to every coin" rabbit hole.

White papers are intense and educational pieces of long-form content. Place these pieces behind a gateway and feel free to send them to people in a Mofu nurturing cycle. Make sure to test how much data you can ask for in exchange for viewing a white paper. In some heavy B2B industries, you can ask for a lot. In the B2C world, it may be more difficult to garner a lot of information in exchange for a white paper.

After Bofu

Another area where brands differ greatly is what happens after viewer engagement in Bofu content, as well as when they exit the funnel completely. Some brands wait until the moment that a lead asks to be contacted with more information on a specific solution. Others want that hand off to happen after a certain amount of content is viewed.

You need to work closely with your sales team to develop a service-level agreement (SLA) as to when this pass will happen organically and automatically. What would make a lead a marketing qualified lead (MQL)? Essentially, it's a lead that marketing has qualified as ready for sales. The marketing team's stamp has been affixed.

Also, in the SLA you'll need to define the process for a sales team member to further qualify a lead as a sales qualified lead (SQL). This is the sales team affixing their stamp on this lead as an actionable lead for a sales member to potentially sell.

If used properly, all these pieces of content can move strangers into visitors, leads, MQLs and SQLs. Engaging in certain types of content will prove levels of interest in your brand and your solutions. When you skip steps, you can hurt the potential of that lead by moving someone through the funnel at your chosen speed and not by their level of interest. You should only skip steps at the potential buyer's request.

Our friends at the beginning of this section seemed to be trying their hand at moving people from the top to the bottom because it serves their business interest. This is not an uncommon approach, but it's also not a commonly successful one.

Passenger Vehicle Driver

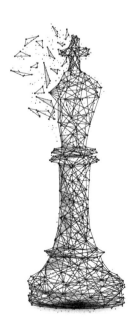

haven't developed a joy for watching auto racing like my buddy Connor. He seems to particularly like Formula One racing.

Now, Connor isn't what I would call the key demographic for auto racing. He's a writer. He has a Master in Fine Arts degree. He plays these sweet ballads—that, in my head, are for his wife—on his acoustic guitar that are calming and touching. He's not afraid to be vulnerable, or to readily share his emotion and his time. He's my fraternity brother. He's a bit of a nerd, but so am I. He's also the editor of this book, so I should add that he is one of the best writers I have ever had the pleasure of reading. He may even be the best writer period. This point can neither be confirmed nor denied. Thanks, Connor.

But what do you think of when I say, "What does a typical auto racing fan look like to you?" Does the person have a mustache? A bit of a beer belly? Is he a he? Does he spend his weekends camping in a recreational vehicle adorned with American flags draped from the retractable awning? This description is of another one of my fraternity brothers, Shaun. He's an auto racing fan, as well as an American Naval hero, but I'll save that story for another book.

In the end, it doesn't matter what a person looks like or which demographic boxes they check when it comes to enjoying something. Enjoyment is derived from the specifics of your personality. Your personality is a concoction of your actions and beliefs and words. These things make up your behaviors and your behaviors hint at your motivations. Now we're marketing.

CONTENT MARKETING IS NOT A VOYEURISTIC SPORT

Content doesn't perform out of fandom, nor does it from your desires for it to be famous, nor how great you think it is. It's not like watching basketball or football. You can't yell your will at it from the stands and hope to affect the outcome. No matter how many people you gather together to yell the same words, you'll not hype up your content to collect a win. Content has no home-field advantage. You've got to climb behind the wheel and take the content where you want it to go.

The work doesn't end when you finish writing. That's just the art part; now comes the science.

You must be an active participant in the performance of the art you've created.

RACE CAR METHOD

The race car intro to this section is deeper than just an opportunity for me to plug a couple of my friends. It stands for a method of content distribution that I've used for years, and it's an easy way to keep focused on the larger picture of content marketing.

Side note: The idioms and analogies throughout this book serve a substantial purpose. Content marketing is a very big thing to wrestle even for the most apt of us. For me, taking the first step on a new project can seem unbearable when knowing the hugeness of the entire venture. These idioms and analogies help make big things very simple. They're like my personal content marketing guidelines. When I'm lost or feel alone in a project, I fall back on the simplicity of each step. If it can be summed-up in an idiom, then it's not that big, now is it?

There is an idiom that I use to describe how these idioms work:

Don't let the hugeness of a thing stop you from taking the first step. The only way to shorten the distance between you and your goals is to take that small first step toward it.

Back to content marketing…

The race car method consists of three parts:

1. **Passenger:** Think of the content itself as a passenger in a race car. Maybe you're a fan of heist stories. I like Michael Crichton's *The Great Train Robbery* myself. In that case, it can be the loot. Nonetheless, it's the thing of value that you're trying to intentionally get somewhere.
2. **Vehicle:** You have a plethora of vehicles to choose from to get your passenger to your destination. Not all are going to be speedsters. Some may be no more than the soles of your shoes. These are content distribution channels. There are many and each of them operates differently—with various strengths.
3. **Driver:** That's you! There must be someone in control and operating the strategy to achieve the desired outcome.

You must be an active participant in the performance of the art you've created.

Passenger

Yes, content is king. It's the most important factor in the performance you seek.

In recap:

You must create your own art. Fabricate nuance through word choice, dripping with voice that's on brand and builds an emotional connection with the reader. Yadda, yadda, yadda.

And no matter the ideal demographic for auto racing fans, anyone can enjoy great content.

However, there are also pieces to the puzzle that live deeper than the superficial entertainment you display on the screen. You know them to be the keys to SEO. Your hyperlinks, keyword targeting, domain strength, et cetera.

As mentioned previously, the keys to great content are revealed through the habits of the writer. You'll need to repeat your efforts and practice them thoroughly. Practice doesn't make perfect in content marketing. PERFECT practice makes perfect. Get it right every time.

Most common types of passengers:

- Blogs and owned articles
- Whitepapers
- Case studies
- Press releases
- Guest or ghost articles
- Testimonials
- Videos, all types
- Memes
- Anything you create

Vehicle

Let's imagine that you have a parking lot filled with vehicles to choose from. Which do you pick? Do you go for the race car? The Lamborghini? Maybe you want to ride in style and not so much speed. How about the Aston Martin? What about the old-stand-by manual bicycle? It's more work, but it's a lot more efficient. Plus, you grow as you go. Muscle builds and you go faster. You learn.

There are no wrong choices when considering a vehicle to drive your content to the finish line of performance. However, there are results. Which means there are failures. That failure isn't in the vehicle itself, but it could be in the combination you created. Maybe that passenger didn't belong in that vehicle. It was designed for a long, slow steep and not bang-up speed.

What's hot and new doesn't mean it'll work for you. But it's worth a try. Apply what you know to be true about your personas and their behaviors. Would someone who is consuming content in a nonchalant and quick manner want to download a whitepaper? So maybe you don't put that whitepaper in the social media vehicle. Maybe that whitepaper is better moved through an email workflow that measures heightened levels of interaction to inevitably lead to a Bofu offer of some sort.

Everybody can't play monopoly with the race car. And those who do don't have any better chances at winning. Sometimes, the thimble wins for no other reason than who chose the piece, their behaviors and motivations.

Most common types of vehicles:

- Social media in all forms
- Organic search engines
- Forums
- Press release networks
- Referral websites
- Partner websites
- Review websites
- Paid search engines
- Display ad networks
- Email
- Any place where you post your works

Driver

The one wildcard variable in the performance of content is you. The quality of the content is on you, but even if you've written or designed a masterpiece, you still need to pick the right vehicle to get the content out into the world. Then, when that's all done, you need to put on your spectacles and your nerd cap and become a scientist.

If you're lucky, your brand has a stable of people who analyze the performance of your content, but it's unlikely, and even if you do, you still need to be active.

It's your job to shepherd your content from start to finish. You need to make sure it gets published. You need to make sure it has proper creative. You need to track the performance of the various vehicles. And you need to be responsible for the performance of the art you create.

Most Common Drivers:

- YOU
- Content mangers
- Content distribution specialists
- Advertising specialists
- PPC or paid search specialists
- Marketing executives
- Social media managers
- Guest writers and content partners
- Anyone who analyzes, tracks or posts your work.

DETOURS

As your vehicle heads toward the finish line, you'll likely encounter roadblocks. These will manifest as dips in performance, snags in distribution and possibly even negative reactions by your audience. Even if you have the aforementioned stable of content scientists, you need to be aware of potholes and try to predict them.

Look as far ahead as possible and think through the likely hiccups with the content you've written and the distribution channels you've chosen.

You can create alternate content to plug into a piece if your original content is rubbing your audience the wrong way. Or you can be prepared to work up a follow-up email with a new subject line for your emails that aren't supplying good open rates. Every small tweak you make may only increase the performance of your content by a few percentage points, but in content marketing world, those points matter greatly. Extrapolate that increase in performance over hundreds of pieces of content and many months, and you'll notice exponential growth.

The more active you are in nurturing your content throughout its journey the better the results will be for you, your audience and your company.

Value Proposition

Out here in this darkness we call content marketing, it can be easy for us to get downtrodden. There aren't very many lighthouses among the fog, and it makes it quite difficult to find sure footing on solid ground.

What does that even look like?

A champion for your cause among the purse string grippers? A supervisor that will listen?

I'm completely in tune with the fact that my circumstances are far from average. I started my career as a copywriter for a company that greatly valued content marketing, and today I find myself with a company that seemingly hired me in part due to my content marketing experience.

However, it's not all rainbows over here. There are times when I proudly walk into meetings and lay my fortunes, and that of my team's, on the line because I believe so strongly in the value of how we're using our precious work hours. And during those months that we come up short of our goal, I have to question my strategy. But that's what marketing is: strategy, action, outcome, question, adjust.

Recently, such an occurrence happened. I was chatting with a coworker in that humbling way we all approach bragging, and I brought up how proud I was of our team this year. We produced over 100 pieces of content with a slim budget. In 12 months, we created more content than the company created in the previous 6 years combined.

His response was a stern, "So what?"

He wasn't purposefully being crass. He was being honest. What does it matter if we've produced more content in a certain period? That's just workload. What does it mean?

I had a retrospective moment then, and I didn't immediately answer him. We were actually out at a bar and the mood to that point was celebratory. Our sales team had announced that they reached their annual goal 3 months ahead of schedule and my team was at 98% of our annual goal at the same time. However, we hadn't reached the most important company goal: revenue.

The conversation had a negative tone from that moment forward and, several beverages later, I was quietly moving into a depressed mood.

As marketers, we're the main force in driving new revenue for a company, and over 100 people's jobs depend on us performing at my office. And things change throughout the year. We acquired two companies, priorities shift and now your starting goal is just a number and not always a direct indicator of companywide success.

I got to my hotel room that night, and sitting on my bed, I grabbed my computer and started with my response to that question, "So what?"

And here is what I have.

CONTENT MARKETING IS AN ASSET

I did two things that night. I wrote up 3 campaign concepts that could be executed in the remaining three months of the year to reinvigorate our lead generation, engage potential customers in a valuable way with our brand and to hit a specific customer goal.

This was my way of accepting the premise of, "So what?" I was mad and then I was a mad man as I whipped up a way to show proof of concept to that question and hopefully drive up some revenue in the last tick of the year. Because yeah, "So what?" is true. Writing 100 pieces of content doesn't put money in the pockets of all those people at the company that depended on us this year. But long-term it certainly will.

I'm sure of it because content marketing is an asset.

The digital conversion cycle goes like this:

1. Someone sees your brand online.
2. They click on it.
3. They view the website.
4. They are convinced on the website to seek more info.
5. They fill out a form.

Sure you can hope people just type in your URL out of the blue because of some offline prompt, but how likely is that?

My father used to say, "Why don't you hope in one hand and shit in the other? Tell me which one fills up first."

I'm not a fan of comparing content marketing to excrement—although I can say some content I've read over the years showed a stark resemblance of such matter—but this idiom holds up.

Hope is not a strategy.

Content marketing helps distribute your brand in a valuable way to the world. If well-written, it'll drive both website visits and conversions.

You need visits to get leads and you need leads to get sales. It's that simple.

The more traffic you create, the more leads you can provide your sales team. You can't do the second without the first.

Moreover, content marketing drives return visitors more than any other type of marketing channel. People truly engage when they find that your brand offers a solution to what they were searching. SEO is a magnet for return visitors and return visitors typically convert at about twice the rate as new visitors.

In the 12 months since starting a vigorous content marketing campaign for my brand, we've gone from about 8,000 organic visits a month to peaking over 300,000 during some months. Our average over the last 12 months is about 260,000. That's an average increase of over 250,000 visits a month.

Just our new blog and landing pages pulled in over 1,200,000 visits the company didn't have the previous year. It also led to about 0.11% of all those visits converting at least once. Some converted multiple times and eventually became customers. That's revenue added to the company's bottom line that wasn't there last year. That's "So what?"

SEO, and content marketing more broadly, is about the long play. It adds value over time. It's like a drip that slowly fills a bucket, but only if that drip has the potential to increase in force over time as well. Before you know it, you're filling a bucket a day.

Content marketing is your company's lead generating 401k. Interest compounds, but you still need to feed it regularly.

SELLING CONTENT MARKETING

It's a huge task to convince the decision makers for your brand that content marketing is an endeavor to embark upon. You need objective facts. You need a chance to show proof of concept, and furthermore, a barrier of entry that isn't a huge sacrifice for the company. They need to believe.

Not an easy task to overcome out here in the darkness.

So here you go. Here is my contribution. I hope the following serves as at lease a flashlight as you wonder through the darkness toward your end goal of providing value through content marketing.

Step 1: Research

Get your facts together and make sure they are objective and not based on your feelings. Have data or a reference for everything you uncover.

First, find out where you are today. Go to some of the online tools to see how you rank in SEO traffic and keywords compared to your competitors. Companies like SpyFu and Moz are fantastic places to start. They can offer you some great charts and graphs that visually represent how you measure up.

Then do some research into the keywords and phrases that are driving people to your website now. Do the same for your competitors. Are you getting beat? Are you close to ranking near the top in some search terms, but you're not quite there? Are there terms that you should definitely be ranking on, but you're not? What are the things people are searching for in the larger universe of your industry? Look at your personas and try to find out what their concerns are. What are they specifically looking for online?

Look at your current traffic more broadly. You can find a lot of this data using Google Analytics. For the very green artists out there, Google Analytics is completely free and they even have a plethora of tools for self-education on both terminology and how to use the product.

Pull all this data together in a comprehensive document, but make sure to have a synopsis at the very beginning. Create a thesis statement and provide bulleted info of the most important pieces. Executives are busy–they must prioritize their time. You should feel confident that if they review just the synopsis, your key point will be driven home.

Step 2: Paint the Picture

In this section, we need to show the decision makers at your company where you want to eventually be. This is your vision. You're an artist, so use your skills to lay out that landscape with happy little birds.

Find some brands that you'd like to emulate. Here is a list of a few of my favorites:

- REI Co-op Blog
- Air BnB Blog
- Disney Blog
- HubSpot Blog
- Moz Blog

Take a moment to notice a common thread between these blogs. None of them are directly about their product. They are about the people that enjoy their products. They target their personas and they aren't trying to tell the company's story, no. They want to tell the story of the people that use their products. And it works.

If it's available, show some examples of brands in your industry doing this well. Or find brands outside of your industry that have the same target demographic that you do. Show how this concept works with the very people that buy your products today.

If you can, provide a vision of what the end product will look like. Work with a graphic designer to actually build some wire frames and graphically show your vision.

Navigate the flow your visitors will take when enjoying your brand new content marketing machine. Show areas of value for them and how your brand will be positioned in their eyes.

Also, make sure you show the path for the visitors to convert into leads. That can be a button to subscribe to content or a chat box at the bottom of the screen. There are dozens of conversion tools to be used on any site. It'll be important to show your executives that there is a way to generate leads and revenue through content and that it's not just writing content about your products.

Again, like in the first section, make a synopsis page with a thesis statement and some bullets. Feel free to throw some of the beautiful art you've created in there, too.

Step 3: The Journey

Here it is: the ask. To this point, we've covered the scientific truth surrounding content marketing through your research, and we've shown how art can help drive value through painting a picture. Now it's time for the final component of marketing, selling.

You might be thinking, "David, I'm on the marketing team, not the sales team." Well, KAREN, first, I'd like to say welcome back from vacation. Oh, you didn't go on vacation. Damnit, KAREN! I'm giving up on you. Just listen up.

We all sell in some fashion. You need to sell this artistic science project we call content marketing. And you're going to do that through presenting an organized approach to a solution they know is grounded in a foundational truth.

You need to show your executives how you plan to take your brand from where you are today to the brand vision you've laid out.

Outline the type of content you want to produce. Make sure to sprinkle in a bunch of opportunities to tell the story of your current customers. Plan testimonials, both in copy and video. Because your executives know that is why people buy today, because they heard about your brand from some raving fan.

Also, add content that will provide value to your personas as they ask questions that pertain to your product universe. If your company sells cruises, then write content about the best ways to destress during your lunch break at work. If you sell financial software for fraternities and sororities, then write content about the top 5 internships for juniors in college.

Make an editorial calendar and commit to 12 months of producing content on a regular tick. Add content distribution channels and an example posting schedule, too.

Also, make sure you have a list of the target keywords you want to go after and how much search traffic each of those terms gets every month. That'll perk up an executive's interest when they hear the opportunity to capture that much additional traffic.

If this is going to cost money, which it likely will, be prepared to answer those questions, as well. Don't shy away from the costs; own it. Factor in freelancers for both content and graphics if need be. And don't forget about development costs for your site if that needs some work, too.

This is the last time I'll mention it; make a synopsis.

Your Website Is an Asset, Too

Just like the computer you use at work and the desk you sit at, like furniture, your website is an asset. Many companies have even taken to capitalizing this expense to save money on their operating budgets. If this sounds like gibberish to you, no worries. Do a little research into the practice of capitalizing expenses and depreciating costs over a period of time.

The reason this is important is because it shows the value of the site. It really is a business asset. It drives reoccurring revenue and it's fairly predictable over time.

Content marketing will allow you to produce leads, sales and even revenue if you keep at it. Also, it gives you a large swatch of data about the people you engage. If you're using a good content management system, you can track the visitors and leads on your site over time. You'll see all the pages they've visited, the places they've converted and your sales team can use that data to better sell a meaningful solution to the potential customers they engage.

In the end, if you do your work and you attack the question "So what?" with your best efforts and still come up short, feel free to use my success as an example. Say, "Hey, look at this guy over here. He sold medical treatments to terminally ill patients through Facebook using content marketing. He drove up his company's organic traffic 31 times higher in 12 months."

And, if you think it'll help in the slightest, reach out to me. I'd be more than happy to help you reach your goals. You don't have to be out here in the darkness alone.

Closing

This isn't the end—it's a waypoint.

I'm in my eighteenth year of studying creative writing. It goes all the way back to when I was 14 and wrote the Austin Boys series mentioned in the introduction of this book. Back then, writing served me as a mystical departure from reality. A reality that I desperately wanted to change and was so very successful in doing so thanks to those stories.

Eighteen years ago, I discovered two foundational truths. The first was that, through writing, we can fabricate emotion in a place void of such things. We can create an entire universe that is only limited by our imagination. The emotions we feel when we read and write are among the few immortal things we can imprint on this world. I read a Junot Diaz quote recently that stated, "The half-life of love is forever." And eighteen years ago, I wondered upon the truth that all emotion we endure through the practice of writing and reading has an equal shelf life. We can lift those feelings off the page and carry them with us into reality to be called upon in those moments where we find ourselves in a vacuum of such nourishment.

This foundational truth is why I became a writer.

The second foundational truth was less discovered in that time, but planted as a seed and nurtured ever since. That truth is that I will never find an end to my journey. There is no pinnacle at the end of my summit. There are valleys and peaks, no doubt, but no final resting place of perfection. I've been studying writing for eighteen years and I have not yet stopped learning. I'm constantly surprised by new foundational truths that pop up in my own personal ethos and various other places when I read, listen to and watch other people on their own journeys.

I used to think there was some place or enlightened state that if I worked hard enough and enough people said "yes" to my crazy ideas, I'd find it. And that this place would wrap its loving arms around me and a feeling of complete belonging would consume me.

Nah.

But without any question, I've seen those moments. They've come upon me when I engage others in spirited debate. I've felt it having conversations with my good friends Connor, Cameron and Tony, all of whom I've enlisted to help me with this book. I've had those moments working with my past teams, my current team and all my supervisors in between. I've also experienced these moments through political discussion with my brothers Geoffrey and Tyler. And in all of these moments, I've found a common thread: I often don't feel as good when I am trying to convince someone of my point than I do when they convince me that I'm wrong. And I think it's because none of us have ever learned anything by being told something we already know.

Between these moments, I've traversed some gigantic valleys—both personal and professional. There have been challenges that, in truth, have consumed far more of my time than those pinnacle movements I've experienced. The total tonnage of failure I've endured in the eighteen years I've been studying writing would topple any man-made scale when measured against my successes. And that's exactly the way I want it to be forever.

For what is the value of success if that's the norm or even the favorite to win?

Life has value because it is finite. Art has value because life is finite. And success has value because it is a shining pinnacle surrounded by valleys of failure.

My personal heaven (if it works that way; I really have no way of knowing) would begin with my ascension to the all-knowing being and said being pulling me aside and saying, hand on shoulder, "Listen, David, We're all happy you're here, you know? It's like, we've been watching, and well, you're great. All of that aside, we've got this problem and we're wondering if you wouldn't mind taking a look at?"

Paradise found.

THE TRAIL BEHIND US

During the journey that was absorbing the pages herein, we've chatted through some of content marketing's fundamental pillars. You've humored me and I hope to have supplied the same to you. Here's a quick recap:

Marketing Is Where Art Meets Science

In marketing, artists are given the chance to create something that impacts the lives of viewers immediately and deeply. It can drive emotion just as a piece of fiction or a painting can. All of this can be measured in a microscopic way. And all this emotion can be returned to the artists. And they can build the foundation of a career upon it.

Voice and Tone Are Different but Not Against One Another

As a content marketer, you can leverage your voice as the feeling of a piece. Slap your love on your writing. It doesn't matter who your audience is, they'll enjoy beauty when they see it. Give them what makes you unique as an artist and writer. Don't devolve to the average. Elevate the reader to be the exception.

Think of brand tone not in a negative way, but as a challenge. You're challenged to make a piece of art that is contextually relevant and is simultaneously beautiful and fulfills the tone of your brand. Oh, and if it converts people, that's great, too.

Three Es

Your target as a content writer should be to create value in others' lives. You can do this through writing content that is entertaining—gives the readers excitement to turn the page; educational—causes them to learn, acknowledge and reflect in ways that they previously have not; and engaging—gives the reader a feeling of urgency to act upon this new piece of value they hold.

Personas

Personas are a further drilldown of people in a demographic. If the demographic is a cloud, then personas are the snowflakes. They are unique, yet derive from a common place.

Behaviors, and the motivations that drive them, will always trump what demographic data predicts. The essence of the persona concept is that you should never discount the raw power that rests within content that is written directly to a unique individual with an intentional shared emotional experience in mind.

Advocate Marketing

No executive will shy away from someone who says, "I'm going to take all the reasons why people buy your products today and multiply those efforts." Curating those word-of-mouth experiences, and digitizing referrals so that more people can learn about the great things your brand is doing, will be a winning formula for any content marketer.

"SEO It"

Love is a verb and so is SEO.

Optimizing a site for organic search is a behavior and not a gimmick.

Just like love, it takes time to perfect and it needs to be maintained, reinvented and invigorated on a regular basis. You need to keep at it and never be fully satisfied or complacent.

SEO means being committed to form, technique and due diligence. It means checking every box on the SEO checklist every time you produce a new piece of content. It means distributing that content into the world. It means maintaining that content long term instead of hitting publish and walking away. It also means writing a piece of art that fits snuggly into the emotionally empathetic box we call conversion.

All Shapes and Sizes

Think of the marketing funnel like a tornado. When you start to gain momentum with your content, you'll suck more and more people into the funnel. Once someone enters the funnel, they cannot escape. You have a plethora of tools at your disposal when trying to move individuals through your marketing funnel. Be mindful of how and with what someone must engage to move down the funnel. Position the right type of contextually written content in the right place and you loosen some people down to the all-powerful bottom of the funnel.

Passenger, Vehicle, Driver

Passenger: Think of the content itself as a passenger in a race car. Maybe you're a fan of heist stories. I like Michael Crichton's *The Great*

Train Robbery myself. In that case, it can be the loot. Nonetheless, it's the thing of value that you're trying to intentionally get somewhere.

Vehicle: You have a plethora of vehicles to choose from to get your passenger to your destination. Not all are going to be speedsters, and some may be no more than the soles of your shoes. These are content distribution channels. There are many, and each of them operates differently–with various strengths.

Driver: That's you! There must be someone in control and operating the strategy to achieve the desired outcome. You must be an active participant in the performance of the art you've created.

Value Proposition

Content marketing will allow you to generate leads, sales and even revenue if you keep at it. It gives you a large swatch of data about the people you engage. If you're using a good content management system, you can track the visitors and leads on your site over time. You'll see all the pages they've visited, the places they've converted and your sales team can use that data to better sell a meaningful solution to the potential customers they engage.

Through good data integrity, you should be able to prove how much end revenue can be expected when you're given money to spend on content marketing.

WHAT'S AHEAD OF US

You've been good company.

We are no longer two wandering souls standing at opposing beachheads and yelling our known truths into the dark abyss. We now stand together. And the light of our truths and the illumination of our spirits have enticed the sun to rise. Now we stand on the beach just as before and shout our truths together. Maybe your truth will teach me something new and maybe mine will be new to you. And although we will be undertaking the same act of yelling straight into the wind, at least now, through our congenial minds, we can see what's in front of us and begin to chart our course.

Please use the examples in this book as political currency in expanding your efforts. Use it as proof of concept for a supervisor that is cautious about spending time and resources on content marketing. In heated marketing debates, slap this book down on the conference table to silence the spirited throngs. Give this book to a co-worker, classmate or friend.

And when you're in a corner and you're feeling alone, please know that you're not. You're a member of a very exclusive club, a writer's club. One where the cost of admission is seeking opportunity through your art.

Finally, if your corner is one of those that we've all faced at a time, where encouraging words and distant friends provide no comfort, reach out to me.

I'll chat with you. I'll talk to your supervisor. If nothing else, let's just yell in the dark together.

You can reach me at ContentWriterWorkshop.com

David J Ebner

Made in the USA
Middletown, DE
21 February 2022

61595826R00066